EVANGELISTIC
SERMONS
of
Clovis G. Chappell

EVANGELISTIC SERMONS
of
Clovis G. Chappell

ABINGDON PRESS
Nashville • New York

EVANGELISTIC SERMONS OF CLOVIS G. CHAPPELL

Library of Congress Cataloging in Publication Data

CHAPPELL, CLOVIS GILHAM, 1882-1972.
  Evangelistic sermons of Clovis G. Chappell.
CONTENTS: Great things.—His thrilling program.
—Bought with a price. [etc.] 1. Evangelistic sermons.
2. Methodist Church—Sermons. 3. Sermons, Ameri-
can.
BV3797.C554   269'.2   73-320

ISBN 0-687-12182-5

MANUFACTURED BY THE PARTHENON PRESS AT
NASHVILLE, TENNESSEE, UNITED STATES OF AMERICA

Preface

Through a crowded lifetime of over ninety years, over seventy of them spent in preaching in churches large and small, Clovis G. Chappell never tired of preaching the unsearchable riches of Christ.

For many years there has been a growing number of requests for a collection of evangelistic sermons such as this. Following his death on August 18, 1972, these sermons were selected from among the many hundreds that he published and preached to congregations all over this land.

In one of these sermons it is said, "Wherever Christ has his way, he does great things." May great things continue to be done wherever this victorious word is preached.

The Publishers

Contents

GREAT THINGS

*Go home to thy friends, and tell them how
great things the Lord hath done for thee.*

MARK 5:19

The story of which this text is a part has certain details
that are thoroughly bewildering. Some of its language
sounds like a foreign tongue to our modern ears. But we
must not allow this fact to blind us to its central message.
This queerness as to details has to do with the nonessentials
of the story, rather than with its essential truth. It has to
do with the setting of the jewel, rather than the jewel itself.
And there is real jewelry here, and that of priceless worth.
This story tells what Christ did for a poor demented wreck
in the long ago. It tells also what he does today for the
soul that gives him a chance.

He does "great things"! I like that word. There are many
who seem to think that our religion has in it more of
weight than of wings; that, at best, its benefits are rather
paltry and worthless trifles. But, in reality, these seeming
trifles are the great things, the priceless things, the supreme
things. "Tell how great things the Lord hath done for
thee." Have you such a story to tell? Is there anything
taking place in your life day by day that can only be
described by this word "great"? If there is nothing, then
you are not claiming your spiritual birthright. If there is
nothing, then your religion is not doing for you what God
intended that it should do. But this is not the fault of your

9

Lord, nor is it the fault of the church. It is your own fault. Wherever Christ has his way, he does great things. Such was the case here. Such has been the case throughout the centuries.

I

Look at this man as Jesus found him. The description given of him is so clear that it would seem to have come from the pen of an eyewitness. The keel of the boat in which Jesus is sailing has hardly touched the shore before a ghastly figure rushes out from one of the tombs. He is wearing practically no clothing. He is disheveled and unkempt. To his wrists and ankles probably still cling the fragments of fetters with which men have vainly tried to bind him. He is a poor half-mad creature with whom we feel little kinship. But when we face the facts, we are made to realize that we have much in common. Of course, we are far more sane than he, far more decent and respectable. Yet we differ from him in degree rather than in kind. This we realize as we study his story. What was the matter with him?

1. He was a divided personality. When Jesus asked him his name, he gave a ready answer: "My name is Legion." That is, he was not one, but many. He was not so much a personality, as H. G. Wells would say, as a battleground. He was at war with himself. He was being tugged in a thousand different directions. A thousand different impulses and passions were warring within his soul. We meet such divided and disintegrating personalities today in the psychopathic wards of our hospitals. But we do not find them there alone. We often meet them as we mingle with our fellows. We sometimes even meet such as we live with

ourselves. Of course, this inner conflict is far less pronounced with some than with others. But all of us know something of the tragedy of a divided personality.

The truth of this is emphasized by modern psychologists. They tell us, for instance, that we are possessed of a conscious and a subconscious mind. In the subconscious mind are the driving instincts that have come to us from our ancestors. These instincts are without conscience. They have no moral sense. They seek their gratification, the pleasure of their own fulfillment, with not the slightest attention to the question of right and wrong. But in the conscious mind there is a sense of oughtness. Here is that which makes us say, "I owe" and "I must" or "I must not." Therefore, the conscious mind rises up against the subconscious. Our ideals fight with our instincts. Our higher self battles with our lower self. Hence we become divided personalities, incarnate civil wars, victims of the direst of all conflicts—the conflict within ourselves.

The writers of the Bible discovered this long before the birth of modern psychology. Here is a man, for instance, who is conscious within himself that he fears the Lord. He is a man of piety and prayer. Even now, he is upon his knees with his face turned wistfully toward the heights. But there is another self within him that refuses to kneel. There is another self that jeers and sneers while the higher self seeks to pray. It is out of the agony of this conflict that he cries to God. For what does this earnest soul make request? What is his prayer? This: "Unite my heart to fear thy name." He has a fear of the Lord that is altogether genuine. But, in spite of this, he is conscious that he is only halfhearted in his fear. He is, therefore, praying for a unified personality, a wholehearted devotion to God.

Here is another man who is also deeply religious. But

he seems more sensitive to the lure of evil than to that of good. He is more conscious of the call of the depths than the call of the heights. He has a keener sense of his baser self than he has of his better self. The voices that call to him to take the lower road seem more appealing than those that call to him to take the higher. But, in spite of this, he cannot wholly give himself to the base and to the unclean. He cannot fling himself with abandon away from all that is beautiful and best. He has gone into the far country of his own choice, yet he cannot be at home there. Therefore, he cries, "My soul cleaveth unto the dust: quicken thou me according to thy word." If with one hand he is grasping at the mud, with the other he is reaching for the stars. Therefore, like this demoniac and like ourselves, he is at war with himself.

2. This poor fellow, being at war with himself, was naturally wretched. "Always, night and day," the story says, "he was crying and cutting himself with stones." Always he was fighting himself. Always he was wounding himself. Always he was his own worst enemy. Thus warring against himself, he was a stranger to real happiness. That is ever the case. No divided personality can ever be happy. However beautiful our surroundings, however large our bank account, however great our success, however thunderous the applause that may ring in our ears—if we are at war with ourselves, we are miserable and will continue to be so till our conflict is hushed into peace.

This is not theory; this is experience. Here is a great soul that is in the midst of this age-old conflict. He is lured by the heights. But when he sets out to climb, he somehow gravitates toward the depths. He hates the unclean and solemnly vows that he will never stretch forth his hand to it again. But while his vow is yet upon his lips, he finds himself guilty of the very deed that he has solemnly foresworn. At last in desperation he utters a wild cry that comes to us across the far spaces of the years. It is a cry that was uttered countless millions of times before it became articulate upon Paul's lips. It has been uttered countless millions of times since then. What is this divided man saying? Just this: "O wretched man that I am! who shall deliver me?" It is a cry of sheer agony. It is wet with the tears of frustration and bitter heartache. I read recently of a man in excellent circumstances who committed suicide. The one reason he gave for his rash deed was this: "I am tired of fighting with myself."

3. Then this man, being divided and wretched, was also antisocial. He had separated himself from his fellows. He lived alone. Nobody could live with him. He was too thoroughly disagreeable. Warring with himself, he also warred with his fellows. And that is the case in some degree with all divided personalities. When we get to fighting with ourselves, we tend to fight with everyone else. When we go to pieces and explode over nothing, when we lose our tempers and slam doors and break up dishes, when we unsheath the sword of our tongue and stab right and left, we call it "nerves." We tell how poorly we slept last night, and how badly we feel. But often the real reason is that we lack inward harmony. We are at war with ourselves. Those torn by inward strife are generally hard to live with.

Being unable to live with his fellows, he was equally unable to live for them. He was, therefore, rendering no high service. He was too busy fighting with himself to have any time for the needs of others. In fact he was a liability rather than an asset, a hindrance rather than a help. Instead of making the burdens of others a bit lighter, he made them the more difficult. Inward conflict always

13

prevents us from enjoying that leisure from ourselves that is necessary to our highest usefulness. In extreme cases, it does for us what it did for this demoniac: makes of us burdens rather than blessings; places us among those who lean rather than among those who lift.

4. Finally, this man was rated as an incurable. He had no hope for himself. Nobody had any hope for him. He was beyond help. "No man," the story says, "could tame him." Thus he was, when Jesus found him, divided, wretched, unable to live with and for his fellows. His is an extreme case, I know, very extreme. But there are few of us that cannot recognize our kinship to him. His needs, therefore, are our needs. What Jesus did for him, is what we long that he should do for us. What Jesus did for him, he surely can do for us. He is still able to save unto the uttermost.

II

Now, what did Jesus do for this demoniac?

1. He gave him a unified personality. That he can do for you and me. And we are not likely to reach this high goal except through him. Certainly no man can ever find inward peace by yielding to his baser self. However fully he may seem to do so, he can never quite hush the voices that call from the heights. One of the most heartless women of all literature is Lady Macbeth. It would seem that the fiends had heard her prayer when she prayed that they would take her milk for gall. She could turn a loyal husband into a murdering traitor, seemingly without compunction. She could plot the death of a royal guest with devilish eagerness. She seems so utterly bad as to be past feeling. But such was not the case. In her waking moments, by

sheer force of will, she could hide the terrible war that raged within. But not so in sleep. Then the conflict reveals itself as she seeks to cleanse her bloody hands, crying, "Out, damned spot! out, I say!"

We find the same truth in Jack London's *The Call of the Wild*—the best dog story, in my opinion, ever written. You remember the hero of the story, a splendid Newfoundland, named Buck. Now, Buck was stolen from his home in the States and shipped to Alaska. Here he had to begin life anew. He was no longer a fireside pet. He was in a harsh world where in order to survive he had to learn to live according to the law of the club and fang. He became a husky, the pride of his new master. He was the best and strongest dog that ran the trail. But it came to pass by and by that his master became ill. As a result, Buck had more leisure than was good for him. In his restlessness, he began to make excursions into the forest. At first these were brief, but gradually they became longer. Soon he was a good hunter, amply able to provide his own food. One night while on a hunt, he heard the howl of a wolf. At once his bristles went up. He was prepared to do battle with this wild thing that he felt was a natural enemy.

But as time went on and the master continued ill, Buck became accustomed to these weird howls. One night, therefore, when he came face to face with this wolf whose mere howls had once raised his bristles and made him eager for battle, there was no conflict at all. Instead, the dog and the wolf put their noses together in token of the fact that they had buried the hatchet. Together they trotted through the aisles of the forest. Together they sat upon their haunches and howled to the distant stars as their ancestors had done centuries before. But always, with the breaking of the day, Buck would return home. At last, his master died and the big tie that bound him to the old life was broken. Soon after that, Buck began to run with the pack, seemingly the wildest wolf of them all. Yet, I daresay, he could never quite throw off all restraints of his former life. He could never become completely a wolf. Certainly this is true with ourselves. Therefore, to take the lower road is to be a divided personality to the end of the day.

But if we cannot find a unified personality by taking the lower road, we can find it by taking the higher. Here again we are not talking the language of theory, but of experience. Listen, once more, to Paul's anguished cry: "O wretched man that I am! who shall deliver me?" Who indeed? Is there a satisfactory answer to that pressing question? There is. Paul answers it out of his own experiences: "I thank God through Jesus Christ." "There is therefore now no condemnation," no inner conflict. He has won as we may win, not by fighting against God, but by surrendering to him. This is what our Lord longs to do for every one of us. He gave and gives to those who fully surrender to him a unified personality.

2. Jesus gave to this tempest-tossed man inward peace. This is ever the result when we make our surrender to God full and complete. For when we have peace with God, we have peace within ourselves. Some years ago, I had a good friend, a minister, who made shipwreck of his faith. But, after much inward conflict and much suffering, he turned back to the Christ that he had forsaken. One day in the course of an intimate conversation he told me his experience. "Have you recovered your old joy?" I asked him when the story was ended. "Better than that," he answered, "I have peace." That is our Lord's special legacy to every one of us: "Peace I leave with you, my peace I give unto you." This is one of the great things that Jesus did

and does for those who give him a chance. Every man's religion ought to give him that inward unity that has its issue in inward peace.

3. Jesus enabled this man to live with and for his fellows. He sent him back to the intimate circle of his own family. He sent him to those that we either love the best or hate the most. He sent him back to live with those with whom, till this experience, he could not live. A prominent physician who lives in another city came to see me the other day. He had but one object in his visit and that was to tell me his experience. After lean, gray years, Christ had come into his life. And among the winsome changes that Christ had wrought, this seemed to give him greatest joy: that he had enabled him to rebuild his broken home. And right here is one of the sharpest and highest tests of our religion. Does it make us easy to live with? If we are cantankerous and disagreeable, if everybody is sorry when we come and glad when we go, then however Christian we may think ourselves, we have missed the mark. Here is a test that every man ought to put to his religion: does it enable him to live with his fellows? A real Christian will certainly be able to meet this test.

Not only did Jesus enable this man to live with folks, he also enabled him to live for them. After this experience, this onetime demoniac had enough leisure from himself to care for those to whom he had once been indifferent, to help where he had been only a hindrance. He helped by what he did. He helped even more by what he was. There is no measuring the service that anyone renders out of whose eyes looks the peace of a great discovery. "Go home," says Luke, "and show how great things the Lord hath done for thee." Show by what you do. Show by what you are.

Stanley Jones tells of a physician who found a stray dog with a broken leg. He took that dog to his home, put its leg in splints, and soon it was able to walk again. Then one day the seemingly ungrateful animal disappeared. The doctor was surprised that after so much kindness the dog should leave him. But he was away for just one night. The next morning there was a scratching at the door. When the doctor opened the door, there was the dog whose leg he had healed. But he was not alone. With him was another dog; lame, as he himself had been, but who had come at the invitation of his friend to be healed. It is as we are gripped by a passion to share that we build up our own personality, and the personalities of others, as well.

III

Here, then, are some of the great things that our Lord can do for us. He can give us a unified personality. He can give us inward peace. He can enable us to live with and for our fellows. Of course, we are not claiming that he does all these instantly. But instantly he can make a beginning. How, then, are we to set about the realization of the great things that he longs to do for us?

Our first step is to be converted. That sounds a bit old-fashioned, I know. "Conversion" is a word that has lost caste among church people in recent years. But if it has lost in one group, it has gained in another. When the teachers and the preachers began to forsake it, then the psychologists took it up. Conversion is a fact. We may be born anew. We can be born from above or from below. I have seen both kinds, and so have you. Some time ago I met a girl whom I had known in former years as a beautiful and devoted Christian. She had been a life volunteer.

But how she had changed! Her face was different. There was a different look in her eyes. She carried herself in a different fashion. Her very walk had a swagger about it that was all but vulgar. What was the matter? She had become the intimate companion of a scoundrel, and in his fellowship she had been reborn, born from below.

But it is our privilege to be born from above. To do this, we must change the master passion of our lives from self to Another. We must become Christ-centered instead of self-centered. When Jesus passed by and said to Matthew, "Follow me," instantly he rose up and followed him. That was Matthew's spiritual birthday. That was his first step toward a unified personality. Why was this the case? Because he had found One whom with deeper and deeper loyalty he could call Master. What did Buck need to steady him when the spell of the wild was upon him? It was not a new kind of collar. It was not a stronger chain. What he needed and all he needed was a master. No dog ever arrives without a master, and this is just as true of a man as of a dog. What do you need with your soul as full of jarring discord as clashing instruments played out of tune? You need a master, the Master. Put the baton into his hands and he will change your discord into winsome music:

I walked life's way with a careless tread,
I followed where comfort and pleasure led;
Till at last one day in a quiet place,
I met my Master face to face.

I'd reared my castles and built them high,
Till their turrets touched the blue of the sky.
And I'd vowed to rule with an iron mace—
When I met my Master face to face.

I met Him and knew Him and blushed to see

19

That His eyes in pity were fixed on me,
And I faltered and fell at His feet that day,
And my castles melted and vanished away.

They melted and vanished, and in their place
I saw naught else but the Master's face.
And I cried aloud, "O make me meet
To follow the path of their bruised feet!"

My care is now for the souls of men.
I've lost my life to find it again,
E'er since that day, in a quiet place,
I met my Master face to face.

HIS THRILLING PROGRAM

Ye shall receive power, after that the Holy Spirit is come upon you: and ye shall be witnesses unto me both in Jerusalem, and in all Judaea, and in Samaria, and unto the uttermost part of the earth.

ACTS 1:8

These are the words of our Risen Lord. Having accomplished his earthly ministry before his return to the Father, he gave his parting charge to his followers. Here are our Lord's marching orders for the church of today. Here is his thrilling program for us as individuals and as a group: "Ye shall receive power, after that the Holy Spirit is come upon you: and ye shall be witnesses unto me both in Jerusalem, and in all Judaea, and in Samaria, and unto the uttermost part of the earth."

I

What is the business of the church? What is the business of every member of the church? It is to witness to Jesus Christ. "Ye shall be witnesses unto me." This is the solemn duty and high privilege of every follower of Jesus Christ. To fail to witness is to fail to bear fruit. To fail to bear fruit is to separate ourselves from our Lord as a branch might be separated from the vine. Thus separated, we wither and die.

21

1. We are to witness through what we say. A witness must have some firsthand knowledge. An evangel must have an evangelist. Hearsay evidence may be of value, but it is never of supreme value. Those who witness effectively for Christ must needs have some firsthand knowledge of him whom they seek to commend to others. Without such an authentic word the best of us may fail, while armed with such a word the least promising can win. As a result of the witnessing of an outcast woman, we read this thrilling word: "Many . . . believed on him for the saying of the woman." I believe the most careless will listen to one who possesses a firsthand, authentic word from the living Christ.

The early church was blessed with some great preachers, such as Paul and Barnabas and Apollos. But the fact that Christianity spread over that hard Roman world like a forest fire was due not so much to great preachers as to the personal testimony of ordinary men and women who went out to tell their friends the amazing difference that knowing Jesus Christ had made in their own lives. To this day it is true that one of the most effective ways of winning men and women to Christ is through personal testimony.

Some years ago a former student of mine called to see me. The years had wrought such vast changes in him that I did not recognize him. He was then a promising young physician. In the course of the conversation he asked if I remembered a walk that we took together when he was a schoolboy. I had to answer in the negative. "Well," he replied, "I have never forgotten it. You spoke to me about becoming a Christian. When I returned to my room, I knelt down and surrendered my life to Jesus Christ. I have had a growing experience of him through the years. I became a physician because I believed that thus I could serve him best and would have the best opportunity to give of myself."

These early saints won largely through their personal testimony. That, I repeat, is still one of the most effective ways of winning others to Christ.

2. We are to witness not only by what we say, but also by what we do. We are to let our light so shine that men may see our good works and be led to glorify our Lord. Jesus rebuked certain Pharisees of his day, not because they failed to teach the truth, but because they failed to practice what they preached. They pointed the way to the spring, but they never drank of the water of life themselves. They indicated the road, but they did not have the consecration to travel it. They commended a life that they themselves did not live. They called the stations on the way to the City of God, but failed to visit those stations themselves.

This always spells tragedy. Of course, the best of us preach better than we practice. This is the case because ours is a perfect gospel, and the best of us practice it imperfectly. Yet it is stark tragedy when we do not accept for ourselves the gospel that we offer to others. How futile to commend any treasure to our fellows if we treat that treasure as a trifle! How useless, for instance, to press on others the value of prayer if we ourselves do not pray.

Generally speaking, the measure of our power to help others is the measure of the fullness with which we have accepted help for ourselves. You are eager for your child to love God's Word. You are eager that he hide it in his heart as a help toward living. But do you read it yourself? I confess a deep love for the Bible. It is a love that has grown with the passing of the years. But I first began to love it by hearing it read by my father about the family altar. It was through his reading that I caught the first glimpse of its beauty. How futile to urge your child to attend Sunday school if you yourself do not attend. How vain to proclaim to him the supreme importance of the church if you yourself shunt it to one side and give it only a third-rate place in your own life. What you say of any value is of importance, but what you do about that value is of far greater importance.

3. We are to witness not only through what we say and what we do, but also through what we are. Sometimes what we are contradicts what we say and do. Always it ought to reinforce and make effective what we say and do. One day two men stood in the presence of the court that had sentenced Jesus to death. The men of this court were not disposed to see the best in Peter and John. But though they looked at them through critical eyes, this conclusion was forced upon them: they were Christlike. "They took knowledge of them, that they had been with Jesus." What these men said by their words and deeds was impressive; what they were was yet more impressive.

Henry Drummond tells that in the heart of Africa among the great lakes he ran across black men and women who remembered the only white man they had ever seen before, David Livingstone. He declares further that their dark faces would light up as they spoke of the kind doctor who passed that way years before. They did not understand a word that he spoke, yet they felt the love that was in the heart of him and had never been able to forget him. This only bears out what the same author said to certain missionaries who were going out to work in India and China. "It will take years," he said, "to learn to speak in the different dialects of China and India, but from the moment you land, love will be pouring forth its unconscious eloquence." What we say and do is, therefore, of great importance. What we are is of superlative importance.

We realize this in our own experiences. When the lamp of faith burns low, when there seems hardly a horizon in your life where you might hope for a dawn, where do you turn to have your faith renewed? Speaking personally, I often turn to certain saints whom I have known along the way. "If there is nothing in this gospel," I say to myself, "how am I to account for him or for her? How am I to account for my own father, who lived his life in such a brave, unselfish fashion? There was something about him that I cannot account for except in terms of Almighty God."

Some time ago I went by request to see a young woman who, as a result of an automobile accident, was a hopeless invalid. She was blind; she was paralyzed from her shoulders down. In addition she was in constant agony every moment of her waking existence. She did not mention the fact of her suffering, but when the nurse told me, she overheard. At that she said these amazing words: "You know, I find myself wishing that I might bear the pain of others. I have learned so well how to handle it." I could hardly have believed that she was telling the truth but for the fact that her face looked as if it had sunrise behind it. As I went away, I was sure that there was no explanation of such a radiant personality except a vital faith in God. We are to witness through what we are.

II

Then our Lord tells us the field of operation. Where are we to give our testimony?

1. In Jerusalem and in Judaea. That means we are to witness to the people among whom we live. We are to

witness first of all in our own homes. Here is a place of supreme importance. Here is our supreme opportunity. If we can bear effective witness in our own homes, then we are on the way to the saving of the nation and of the whole world. But if we fail here, we fail everywhere. No church, no community, no nation will ever rise higher than its home life. If we save the home, we save all else. If we fail at home, we fail everywhere.

Our testimony in the home is of supreme importance, not only because the home is the fountain from which flow the streams that make the sea of our national life, but because it gives us our best opportunity to witness effectively. This is the case for the following reasons: (1) A child can be a Christian. (2) A child can become a Christian easier than anybody else. (3) Those who become Christians as children make the best Christians. It is well to bear in mind also that if we fail to win our children while they are children, the chances are that they will never be won. Our first and greatest opportunity, therefore, of bearing witness to Jesus Christ is in our own homes.

To witness in Jerusalem and Judaea is also to witness in our home church, in our community, our city, our state, and nation. We are to witness by being good churchmen and by being good citizens. I have heard people bewail civic and political situations, declare that something ought to be done about these; then, when an election is held and an opportunity is given to banish the evil, fail even to take time to vote. We are to witness, therefore, right where we are. If we fail at the home base, we fail everywhere.

2. We are to witness to the Samaritans. These Samaritans were kinfolks of the Jews. They were a mongrel race, held in great contempt by their Jewish kinfolk. But Jesus was as keenly interested in the Samaritans as he was in the Jews.

He expected that interest to be shared by his followers. Therefore he gave them a commission to Samaria. We too have our Samaritans, our minority groups. We are to witness to them. I have known professing Christians who were ready to contribute liberally to the needs of the Negroes of Africa, but who took no interest in the needs of those who lived in their own community and even worked for them in their own homes. We are to witness to those against whom we might have a natural prejudice.

3. Finally, we are to witness to the ends of the earth. Ours is a world religion. So taught Jesus. He declared that the field is the world. If I did not believe that our Lord cared for all men, I could not believe that he cared for any man. The very heart of our gospel is this: "God so loved the world, that he gave . . ." To assume that God is interested in home missions but not in foreign is to assume that he is lacking not only in heart, but in intelligence.

This is the case because even the blindest can see now how difficult it is for the world to have peace when one half is even nominally Christian and the other communistic. We know now that to be intelligently interested in any one man is to be interested in every man. This is the case because we are all bound together in a bundle of life. It is a heartening fact in these desperate days that the saints have so taken these marching orders of our Lord to heart that ours is now a world church. The one institution that girdles the globe today is the church of Jesus Christ.

But while we are out to save the world, we are not to forget the individual. I have known a few who lost the individual in the mass. They were so bent on building a new world that they seemed to lose sight of the importance of building a new man. It is rather significant that the one group that did most to change the social order in their generation had almost nothing to say about it. These first Christians went out to preach Christ. As they gave their testimony, the words of Isaiah were fulfilled: "The wilderness and the solitary place shall become glad . . . ; and the desert shall rejoice, and blossom as the rose." Age-old evils vanished like mist before the sunrise. This was the case not so much because they preached against these evils as because they won the individual to personal loyalty to Jesus Christ.

III

This, you will admit, is a great program. What of the power to see it through? Is there sufficient dynamic for its accomplishment? If so, where shall we turn for that dynamic? Let it be said at once that our Lord never purposed that we should conquer in the energy of the flesh. No more is it to be the work of God alone. The changing of the kingdoms of this world into the kingdom of our God and his Christ is a cooperative movement. Man cannot do it alone. God cannot do it alone. But God and man working together can accomplish it. Therefore our Lord said, "Ye shall receive power, after that the Holy Spirit is come upon you."

Now, we are prone to rob these words of their simplicity. We are prone to look at the experience here promised as only for abnormal Christians, for certain fanatical disciples who live near the lunatic fringe of religion. But such is not the case at all. This is to be the experience of the normal Christian. Anything less than this is subnormal. This Pentecostal experience is for every man who will meet the conditions. What, then, happened to those who experienced Pentecost?

Suppose we take our eyes off what was incidental and passing about this greatest event in the life of the church, and ask what it did for those who participated in it. What did it do for them? It remade them. Here they were reborn. There are those who will not agree, but I doubt if there was a really regenerated man among the disciples before this experience. Up to this time they followed Jesus, tried in some fashion to imitate him, but now they went out to reproduce him. Being reborn, these Christians came to know their Lord as a present, personal fact in their lives. It was in the power of a vivid awareness of God through the Spirit that these early saints went forth to change the world.

Why, then, are we often so lacking in power as individuals? Why do we have so few churches that are really powerful? I think the answer is right here. It is our lack of wholehearted committal to our Lord and to his program. We cannot expect Pentecostal power if we do not take seriously the program of world salvation for which that power was given. It is just as true now as it was then that wholehearted surrender brings power. When we give, God gives: "We are his witnesses of these things; and so is also the Holy Spirit whom God hath given to them that obey him."

Here, then, is our task. What a majestic adventure it is. What an infinite distance separates it from that sickly conception of Christianity as something that is not worthy of the really strong and brave. Here is an undertaking big enough for the biggest of all big souls. No other task can possibly be so worthy or so urgent. We know now as never before that there is no other name under heaven given among men whereby our world can be saved.

Years ago I crossed the North Sea on the same ship with

a man who was a missionary to China. I did not meet him personally. I was too seasick. This man was said to be more familiar with things Chinese than any other man at that time. Because of this a great oil company sought to obtain his services. It sent a representative to offer him a salary of $10,000 a year. When he refused, the representative went up to $20,000, then to $25,000; then he invited him to set his own salary. In reply this missionary said, "The salary you offered first is large enough; I am making only $1,200 a year. It is not your salary that is too small; it is your job. I have a bigger job than you can possibly offer."

So has every man who takes his Lord seriously, however he earns his living. Ours is the biggest task at which any human soul can work.

BOUGHT WITH A PRICE

*The church of God, which he hath purchased
with his own blood.*

ACTS 20:28

Paul is on his way to Jerusalem. Not being able to visit
the church at Ephesus, where he had labored so sacrificially
and successfully, he did the next best thing. He asked the
official board of that church to meet him in Miletus. When
they had come, the great apostle poured out his heart to
them in a message which is one of the most beautiful and
compelling that St. Luke has recorded for us. This message,
in my opinion, reaches its climax in the words that I have
chosen for my text. Paul appeals to the elders to "feed
the church of God, which he hath purchased with his own
blood."

Instead of "the church of God" the Revised Standard
Version translates this as "the church of the Lord." This
is, no doubt, the better translation. Yet as it stands in the
King James Version, it still holds a profound truth. Since
"God was in Christ, reconciling the world unto himself,"
it comes to pass that Christ on the cross was, in a profound
sense, God on the cross. The church, therefore, that was
purchased by the blood of the Lord was at the same time
purchased by the blood of God.

I

"The church of the Lord, which he hath purchased with
his own blood." This brings us face to face with Paul's

31

conception of the church. It is impossible to read Paul's letters without seeing that he thought grandly of the church. The most heartbreaking memory of his life was the memory that he had once persecuted the church. His most thrilling joy was that it was now his privilege to belong to the church and to help in building it. He fairly taxed his rich vocabulary in an effort to tell his converts and all others of the beauty and worth of the church. Some of these great words haunt us to this day.

For instance, Paul thought of the church of our Lord as a family. It was no ordinary family. It was the very family of God. It was the household of faith.

Again, he pictures the church as a bride. She is no ordinary bride. She is the bride of the world's Redeemer.

Once more, he sees the church as the body of Christ. It is that living organism through which the Lord still speaks his message, still carries on his work of seeking to save that which is lost.

Perhaps his favorite conception of the church was as the temple of the living God. He looked upon each individual saint as a temple indwelt by the Holy Spirit: "Know ye not that your body is the temple of the Holy Spirit?" The church, therefore, is a temple built not of stones, but of individual temples. It is built of the redeemed sons and daughters of God.

In our text Paul speaks of the church as the organization which Jesus Christ has purchased for himself with his own blood. He is affirming that as a group and as individuals we who belong to the church are not our own, but that we have been bought with a price. There are certain supermoderns who seem more horrified than wooed by this so-called doctrine of the shambles. But here one of the most cultured and sensitive men that we meet in the pages of the New Testament or anywhere else affirms that this church to which he belongs has been purchased by the blood of our Lord.

II

Now, whether we are wooed by this conception or repelled by it, it is of the very warp and woof of the New Testament. It is impossible to get rid of it without tearing both the Gospels and the Epistles into shreds. It is impossible to be rid of it without emasculating the New Testament. Paul believed it and rejoiced in it with joy unspeakable. If my text were his only reference to the fact that we have been bought with a price, then it would not be so impressive. But this conception runs through all that he said.

For instance, when he sums up the gospel that he had preached and was preaching, he puts it in these words: "I delivered unto you first of all that which I also received, how that Christ died for our sins according to the scriptures." Again, writing to this same church, he urges, "Ye are not your own. For ye are bought with a price." "You have been bought and paid for" is the way Goodspeed translates it. Again he declares, "We preach Christ crucified, unto the Jews a stumblingblock, and unto the Greeks foolishness; but unto them which are called, both Jews and Greeks, Christ the power of God, and the wisdom of God." "We preach Christ crucified." What impressive words those are! He did not claim to preach about Christ. Anybody can do that. But he proclaimed, heralded, a crucified Christ.

When Paul was in Athens, when he addressed the learned Greeks of the Areopagus, he decided, scholar that he was, that he would speak to these men of the intelligentsia in their own vernacular. He would show them that he too was a man of learning. Therefore he quoted from their own poets as if he himself were an Athenian. But the response of these hearers, who had a passion for newness, was very disappointing. There were few converts.

Therefore, when the great apostle reached his next preaching mission, he gave up the tactics employed at Athens once and for all. He told his hearers that he was determined not to know anything among them save Jesus Christ, and a crucified Christ at that. It was this constant proclamation of Christ crucified that got him into trouble. Writing to the church at Galatia he affirms as much. But he was determined to go on with such preaching because it was his one hope, and the one hope for the world. In this faith he writes, "God forbid that I should glory, save in the cross of our Lord Jesus Christ, by whom the world is crucified unto me, and I unto the world."

In thus affirming that we are bought with a price Paul does not stand alone. That was the faith of his fellow saints. It was the faith of his brethren in the ministry. When the author of the book of Revelation seeks to tell of the immeasurable debt that he and his fellow Christians owe to Christ, he puts it in these words: "Unto him that loved us, and washed us from our sins in his own blood." The writer to the Hebrews believed that there is no entrance into the holiest of all except by the blood of Jesus. The founder of Methodism whispered these great words as he passed into the presence of his Lord. When Simon Peter desired to strengthen the courage of the hard-pressed Christians who were being persecuted and sown broadcast over the earth, he reminded them that they had been redeemed, not by anything so trifling as silver and gold, but by "the precious blood of Christ."

How did these joyous saints come by this conviction? I answer, They came to it by listening to Jesus himself. "The Son of man came not to be ministered unto, but to minister, and to give his life a ransom for many" are the words of our Lord. When he read the Twenty-third Psalm, he saw in the good shepherd a picture of himself. "I am the good shepherd," he declared. What is the difference between the good shepherd and the hireling? The hireling might be willing to do much for the sheep under his care, but he is not willing to pay the last full measure of devotion. But the good shepherd shows his goodness in that he is willing to lay down his life for the sheep.

That scene in the upper room tells the same story. Jesus is celebrating the feast of the Passover with his disciples. During this feast he dares to replace the paschal lamb with himself. As he takes the bread and breaks it, he puts a bit in the hand of Simon, who is soon to deny him; in the hand of Judas, who is to betray him; in the hand of each of the ten, who are to forsake him and flee. And he says to them this word: "This is my body which is given for you." By this he is telling them, "This is myself, my best, my all, given for you. I am seeking to win you at the price of life laid down."

We cannot, I say, get away from this phrase, "which he hath purchased with his own blood," without destroying the New Testament.

Not only is this the case, but we cannot get away from it without giving up that which has been the central hope of the saints through the centuries. Followers of Christ have crossed all seas, penetrated all forests, laid their ashes upon all shores, in order to proclaim this message. They have sung it in hymns, some of which are quite crude. They have sung it also in hymns, some of which are the most majestic in the language. These hymns have through the centuries been stairways on which rejoicing saints have climbed toward God. Where is there a real Christian who cannot join joyously in this great song?

> When I survey the wondrous cross
>   On which the Prince of Glory died,
> My richest gain I count but loss,
>   And pour contempt on all my pride.
>
> Were the whole realm of nature mine,
>   That were an offering far too small;
> Love so amazing, so divine,
>   Demands my soul, my life, my all.

III

What did Paul mean when he said the church was purchased by the blood of Christ? What do the readers of the New Testament mean; what do we mean when we use such language today? Let it be said at once that there is no thought of the commercial in this transaction. I take it that no Christian thinks today that by such language we mean that God bought us from the devil at the price of the death of Jesus. Such a conception is as horrible as it is unreasonable.

If, then, Paul had no thought of a commercial transaction when he spoke of the church being purchased by the blood of our Lord, what, I repeat, did he mean? He meant very much what we mean when we use such language today. This conception has entered into our everyday speech. We hear it everywhere and employ it over and over again.

For instance, some months ago I delivered the commencement address for a certain school. After this address a young man was presented with a scholarship medal. As far as I could see, all that young gentleman had to do to obtain that medal was to arise when his name was called, walk across the platform, and stand still while some official pinned the medal upon the lapel of his coat. But if after the meeting I had reminded this young man of the ease with which he had won his medal, how he had had nothing to do but to walk a few steps and to stand perfectly still, he would doubtless have informed me that what I saw was not the whole story. He would have told me that he had not received the medal as a gift but as a reward. He might have said with truth, "I bought the right to wear that medal by the hard work I did behind the scenes."

More than a generation ago a young woman of natural gifts in the realm of music determined that she would become a great artist and sing at the Metropolitan. By and by she achieved her ambition. She was acclaimed as a brilliant success. But her victory was costly. In her effort to realize her ambition she sacrificed some of her dearest friends. In her effort to win she even gave up the privilege of marrying the only man she ever loved. In fact, so much did she have to sacrifice that the one who wrote her story entitled his book *The Price She Paid.*

James Barrie, in a one-act play entitled *The Will,* shows us the price that one businessman paid for the winning of a fortune. As the curtain rises, we see a delightful young couple in the gloomy office of a London solicitor. The husband is just beginning to prosper. Though he is still young, he thinks it wise to make a will. To this his devoted wife agrees, in spite of the fact that she cannot keep back her tears at the thought of what a will suggests—the possible death of her husband. Though they are far from rich, the generous young wife insists that her husband remember in his will two old maiden cousins who will need all the help he can give. All in all, this solicitor finds the couple so beautifully unselfish and charming that his gloomy office takes on a new and gladsome brightness because of their presence.

Years go by, and the husband and wife are in the office once more. The husband has come to make another will. His wife has come also, not by invitation this time. She has come, as she herself puts it, to see that her husband "does nothing foolish." One of the foolish things she forbids him to do is to leave so much money to the two old maiden cousins. Of course, they are now years older and therefore less able to provide for themselves. But that is none of her business. They really ought to be dead anyway. Therefore she insists that her husband leave a lesser amount to them.

Then more years go by. Once more the husband has come to make a will. This time he is alone. He has prospered throughout the years and is now the possessor of a fortune. But as he faces his lawyer, there is no gladness in his tired eyes, no sunshine in his hard face. Holding a bit of paper in his hand, he spits these words at his lawyer: "My wife is dead; my daughter has run away with the chauffeur; my son is a rotter. On this piece of paper are the names of the men with whom I have fought most savagely for gold. I have won. Make out a will leaving my fortune to them with my respectful curses." He had bought his wealth, but he had bought it at a great price.

When, therefore, the New Testament affirms that we have been purchased by the blood of Christ, it is using language that is at once familiar and true. Jesus has bought us at the price of life laid down.

IV

Why did Paul insist on this doctrine of the cross?

He was insistent because it was Christ crucified who had taken captive his own hot heart. Jesus, who knew men as no other ever did, counted on his sacrificial death as his supreme appeal: "And I, if I be lifted up from the earth, will draw all men unto me." In basing his confidence for the winning of men upon the appeal of the cross, our Lord was altogether right. Through the centuries this strange Man on his cross has cast his spell upon the hearts of all sorts and conditions of men. Love that gives to the uttermost will win when all else fails.

It was this sacrificial love, I repeat, that won Paul and that sent him to give his life tirelessly in the service of others. When I see this man of vast scholarship and ability squandering himself day by day on slaves and ex-slaves and social nobodies, I cannot but be amazed. I watch him going in hothearted earnestness to throw himself away, seemingly with little reward except shame and scars and imprisonment. "Why do you do it?" I ask. "Are you mad?" as Festus once affirmed. "No," he flashes back at me with a ring of joy in his voice. "I am thus giving myself, not because I am mad, but because 'he loved me and gave himself up for me.' "

Thus, when Paul stood face to face with Christ crucified, he surrendered all to him. That is what in our heart of hearts we know we ought to do. That is what we really long to do. Suppose we respond here and now to that holy urge. If we thus respond, this is the wealth that I can promise in his name. If you give him yourself, he will accept you. That is his own word: "Him that cometh to me I will in no wise cast out." Not only will he accept you, but he will remake you and use you for the remaking of others.

THE WORK OF THE EVANGELIST

Do the work of an evangelist.

II TIMOTHY 4:5

I

"Evangelism" is a beautiful word that has lost its winsomeness. Somehow on its journey from the Jerusalem of yesterday to the Jericho of today it has fallen among thieves that have wounded it and stripped it, and departed, leaving it half dead. It takes a rather rash Samaritan, therefore, to dare turn aside to set this poor chap upon his beast and take him to an inn and take care of him. This is especially true because a veritable procession of priests and Levites are passing by, not only refusing to lend a hand, but, we fear, inwardly chuckling at the plight of the poor fellow, and secretly hoping that they are soon to see the last of him.

Now, this has not always been the case. I am not among the ancients, but I can remember when the first day of the revival brought the people together in unusual numbers and with heightened expectancy. And I have seen multitudes come together greatly wondering, saying, "What do these things mean?" because there were big events taking place that could only be accounted for in terms of God. But that is largely of yesterday. The announcement of a revival in the average church is no longer a clarion call for the rallying of the hosts of Zion. It is rather a warning gong that calls, "To your tents, O Israel." Our people, even some of the best, flee for refuge to the security of their homes, or to their cars on the open road. The announcement of a revival today in the average city church would be about as effective in bringing together a congregation as if the pastor were to say, "My brethren, next Sunday we are to have on exhibition in this church some very interesting cases of contagious disease. If you come and bring your families, you may be able to contract one or more of them."

As to just how this change has come about, it is not my purpose fully to explain. Of course, I know the one on whose shoulders we are accustomed to lay the heaviest part of the responsibility. It is upon the professional evangelist. But, of course, no fair-minded man would make a whole-sale condemnation of these ministers. Some of them are the salt of the earth. They are holy men, the latches of whose shoes I personally feel myself unworthy to unloose. But there was a type of which this was not the case. You remember how they used to come with their high-powered methods and their veteran sermons that had done yeoman service in many a hard-fought campaign, but had not grown shorter, but rather longer. For you know an old sermon is a bit like a snowball rolling down a hill—it grows larger all the time, but what it accumulates is generally rubbish. These brethren often had a genius for counting sham results and real money. They reigned as kings for a few days, and then folded their tents like the Arabs and silently went away, leaving us on four flat tires spiritually, and with our spares stolen.

But even for this type of spurious evangelism the evangelist was by no means solely to blame. An equal, if not a heavier, part of the responsibility must be put upon the pastor and his people. Often when we invited the evangelist we did not do so because we were eager for a real refreshing from the presence of the Lord. We were rather seeking a smooth road out of a hard situation. We wanted a million-dollar return on a five-cent investment. We were eager for a bumper crop without giving ourselves to the prosaic task of clearing and breaking and tilling the soil. This counterfeit evangelism, I am sure, has done much to bring the genuine into disrepute.

Then there are those who look askance at evangelism because they feel that it has been too individualistic and has demanded too small a sovereignty over life. But, in my opinion, our lost passion for evangelism is due more to our lost sense of God than to any other cause. "Then said I, Here am I; send me" is the testimony of one who years ago burned with a hot enthusiasm for sharing the blessings that had come into his own life. "Then"—this is a backward-looking word. Upon what does it look? It looks back to the time when Isaiah had seen "the Lord high and lifted up"; to the time when in the light of that vision he had seen himself as a sinner, and had been made clean. The fires of evangelism always burn in hearts that are conscious of the Divine Presence. And when men lose that consciousness, the fires go out.

II

Just what do we mean by evangelism? Its simplest meaning, as you know, is to tell Good News. But to understand it fully we need more than a definition—we need to see it in terms of personality. Let us, therefore, turn to the Supreme Evangelist. Mark, in his romantic and aggressive Gospel, shows him to us with peculiar clearness: "And Jesus came into Galilee preaching the Good News about

God." He told men that they were all the sons of God, that it was every man's privilege to call God "Father." He showed how life's supreme tragedy consists in our effort to be independent toward our Father. That was the tragedy of the graceless laddie of whom we read in the fifteenth chapter of St. Luke. He went away from home, not because he wanted to grieve his father, but because he wanted to be independent of him. But life was transfigured for him the moment he determined to take a son's place in his father's house.

By telling men that they are all the sons of God, he told them the further Good News that they were brothers one to the other. He told them that no man need live as a stranger in this world, that men need no longer glare at each other across frozen chasms of indifference, or fiery chasms of hate—that every man might see in his fellow a brother. And Jesus not only preached brotherhood, but he lived it. He put himself under every man's load. He dined with outcasts. He talked to harlots with the same gracious courtesy that he showed to the purest of the pure. Thus he dug a chasm between himself and decent folks and went to the cross for doing the work of an evangelist.

But after Jesus had been crucified, men who had been baptized into his spirit took up his message. One gifted young man, by the name of Stephen, evangelized so compellingly in Jerusalem that "they were not able to resist the spirit and the wisdom by which he spake." Unable to answer him with words, they mobbed him. But though they stoned the life from his body, they could not stone the radiance from his face: "They saw his face as if it had been the face of an angel." Though they robbed him of his life, they could not rob him of his love. He died with this

Christlike prayer upon his lips: "Lord, lay not this sin to their charge."

Among those having a part in this ghastly crime was a young man who was about the best intellect of his day. He tried to forget the ugly memory by giving himself to an orgy of persecution. But he was never able to brush the beauty of that radiant face from his mind. He was never able to stop his ears to that Christlike prayer. At last, on the way from Jerusalem to Damascus, Paul surrendered and fell upon his face, and cried, "Lord, what wilt thou have me do?" He then rose to his feet to do the work of an evangelist. He, along with certain nameless nobodies, went about over the Roman Empire establishing little "colonies of heaven."

These colonies were made up of men and women who did not fear the world's fears. They were men and women who were not gripped by the world's greeds. They were not divided by the chasms that divided others. The pagan world looked on with wistful wonder and exclaimed, "How these Christians love each other!" And because they wanted to love and be loved, they were drawn into these little groups. Thus the Lord added unto them day by day such as were being saved. And as they increased in numbers, they increased in power. Out from them flowed rivers of living water that had a perfectly amazing capacity for withering all that was selfish and unclean, and for making all that was beautiful to grow. The Roman Empire took knowledge and tried to destroy them. But the more they were killed, the more they lived. At last they became so mighty that they displaced the Roman eagle with the cross. Then they began to fear the world's fears, and to be gripped by the world's greeds. Then the sun went down and the night came on, the night of the Dark Ages that lasted almost a thousand years.

Then centuries went by, and England is in the throes of a terrible reaction from Puritanism. And Christianity seems to many a dead and exploded theory. But one night there came out of a little service in Aldersgate Street a man who declared that he had felt his heart strangely warmed. That man mounted his horse the next day and set out on an evangelistic tour that carried him literally through the century. And out of his hot heart there breathed upon England a veritable Gulf Stream. At the kiss of its warmth the icicles fell from the eaves of the houses, the winter-stripped trees put on their verdant foliage, the flowers bloomed, the birds sang, and the heart stood up in the glad consciousness that God had come. Every reader of history knows today that by far the biggest event of that eventful century was the evangelism of John Wesley and his followers.

III

And now we come to our bewildered and perplexed day. It is a day of cynicism, a day of disillusionment, a day of bitter hunger of heart. Some poet a century from now might sing of large areas of the life of our day:

On that hard pagan world, disgust and secret loathing fell,
Deep weariness and sated lust made human life a hell.

Multitudes are "between two worlds, the one dead, the other powerless to be born." But our desperate need is at once our challenge and our opportunity. Surely multitudes both within the church and out of it are realizing as never before that there is none other name under heaven given among men whereby we must be saved but the name of Jesus.

The call of the hour, therefore, is for the right kind of evangelism. It is only as we evangelize that we shall build up the body of Christ. Doing the work of an evangelist builds up the evangelist himself. There are multitudes even in our churches to whom Jesus Christ is as vague and dim as the shadow of a dream. Is there a roadway to spiritual certainty? I am sure that there is. Jesus is still coming to seek and to save that which is lost. If you and I set out on the same quest, our roads and his are sure to run together sooner or later. We will come face to face with the Christ who is doing what we are undertaking to do. For if any man is willing to do his will, he shall know. We shall also build by capturing from without. It has been my habit through the years to give an opportunity at every service for men and women to make a public confession to Christ. Many times I have called when nobody has responded, but the vast majority of calls have not been in vain.

While seeking the lost, we are to realize that our most fruitful work is not with adults, but with childhood and youth. It is still hard for some to believe this. A fine old gentleman said to me after a service that I had had with the boys and girls, "I do not believe in services of that kind." "Why?" I asked. "Because," he said, "ten or twenty years from now some of those boys and girls could not tell you when they were converted." "What of it?" I asked. "Why," he said, with vehemence, "I would not give the pop of my finger for any man's religion who could not tell you the day and the hour in which he was converted." Now, if you know when you were converted, thank God for it, but remember this: there may be one sitting beside you who is more beautifully conscious of the Divine Presence than you are, who does not know.

When I was a boy, my father gave me a little colt. He gave me that colt the very day it was born. I began at once to get on good terms with it. I would rub its nose and stroke its ears. Now and then I would give it an apple core (if I could spare it). Then at last I dared to mount that colt and go for a ride. Never once did he throw me, or kick me, or paw me. If you had asked that colt three years later, "When were you converted into a work horse?" he would doubtless have answered you in the language of Socrates, "Search me."

But there was another colt about the same age as mine, to which nobody paid any particular attention. One day my father said that he was old enough to be converted into a work horse. Therefore we chased him out of a pasture into the lot, and out of the lot into a stable. We bridled and harnessed him and plowed him beside a maturer horse. Then we unhitched him and let him out to where the ground was soft. We called a friend in whom we had a personal interest and asked him if he would be so kind as to mount. And when he mounted, the back of that colt went up like the apex of an isosceles triangle, and the brother erased himself. Finally, after he had thrown a few more men, after he had torn up one or two pairs of harness and kicked the spatter board out of the buggy, a strong man could drive him provided he was tired. If you had asked him three years later when he was converted, he would have said, "I shall never forget it as long as I live. It was a terrible ordeal." But I submit to you that my colt was broken in a far more normal and a far more natural way. All of which leads me to say that the best field of evangelism is the home, for the only sure way to have Christians is to raise them.

Finally, if we are to do the work of an evangelist, we must be willing to pay the price. Evangelism is costly. There is no twilight sleep process for the bringing of new-born souls into the kingdom. It is only as Zion travaileth that she brings forth sons and daughters. That is the reason that an ease-loving church like ours shies away from it. We do not like to be bothered. The passionate words of the saints sound to us a bit like a foreign tongue: "And now, behold, I go bound in the spirit unto Jerusalem, not knowing the things that shall befall me there; save that the Holy Ghost witnesseth in every city saying that bonds and afflictions abide me. But none of these things move me." And here is rugged John Knox crying, "Give me Scotland or I die." We rather say, "Give me a comfortable bit of Scotland, or I will move." Too few of us believe in evangelism enough to be eager to pay the price. But where the price is paid, results are sure.

Several years ago I was conducting a revival in a little town where there were seven or eight churches that had just enough interest to quarrel among themselves. The meeting was going badly, and I was desperately discouraged. At last I tried to have a testimony meeting, and the testimonies dwindled into discouraging and critical sermonettes. Just as I was preparing to close the service in despair, a gentleman stood up that I came to know intimately, and to honor and love with genuine devotion. His presence was not prepossessing. He was rather shabbily dressed. He used bad grammar. But what redeemed him from common-placeness was a marvelously illuminated face. It looked like it had a sunrise behind it, and you felt yourself almost unconsciously peeking round to see where the light came from.

He turned that wonderful face toward me and said, "Brother, I thank God that things are just as they are." I looked at him in wide-eyed amazement. But he went on to explain: "I love to get in a hard place for my Lord. I love to get in a place that is so hard that there is no chance to get into without you get down on both hands and knees and crawl through to God." I saw that he knew a secret with which I was too little familiar. After this testimony, we dismissed and went home.

In the evening service that followed, the tabernacle was crowded to overflowing. There was a mourners' bench that ran entirely across the tabernacle. It was long enough to have accommodated at least a hundred mourners, though one an inch long would have been long enough for what we had been having. I stepped out on this mourners' bench and began my sermon. I had been preaching only two or three minutes when this brother came and kneeled down beside me, and as he prayed I tried to preach. And, account for it how you may, the atmosphere was utterly changed. I saw strong men come from out the dark to kneel at the altar, but before they could get on their knees they rose into newness of life. "And the place was shaken where we were assembled together, and we were all filled with the Holy Spirit." And it is my conviction that the church will never rediscover the lost secret of its evangelistic power till it learns again the high art of prayer. Let us therefore take to heart the challenging words of our text, "Do the work of an evangelist."

WHEN GOD CAME BACK

And the Lord appeared again in Shiloh.

I SAMUEL 3:21

This is a word to lift the heart and set the soul to dreaming. If we can hear it without a thrill, it is either because we fail to understand or because familiarity has dulled its keen and cutting edge. God has come back. This is the great news that has passed from man to man, from home to home, and from village to village, till all Israel has been filled with a new expectancy and a new hope. The world could not ignore the return of Napoleon from Elba. The record of that return was written in terms of blood and tears. But the record of God's return is written here, as always, in terms of individual and social enrichment.

I

"The Lord appeared again in Shiloh." We can readily see what this word implies. It indicates that God had been away. "Once more the Eternal was to be seen at Shiloh," Moffatt translates it. That indicates that there had been gray days through which he had not been seen. Of course, he had never been absent. In every age he surrounds his people as the waters of the sea surround the vessel. In every age he is infinitely near. In every age he stands at the door and knocks. But so often we fail to recognize him. When we thus fail, God becomes to us as if he were distant or as if he were dead.

50

This absence on the part of God had stretched over a long period. It was three centuries now since the death of Moses. God had illuminated briefly a few foothill personalities during these years. But there had been no mountain peak that had approximated the height of Moses. As long as this great man lived, he had kept alive among his people a sense of God. That was a great tribute they had paid him—all the greater because it was unconscious—when they had said to Aaron, "Up, make us gods, which shall go before us; for, as for this Moses, . . . we know not what is become of him." That is, when Moses had gone, as far as they were personally concerned, God had gone. All they had seen of God they had seen in the personality of their great leader.

II

But now, God had come back. How did God come?

He came through human personality. We are made in God's image. We are made in God's image in that we are persons. We are like God in that we have power to choose, and power to know, and power to love. Since man is kin to God, God can reveal himself to him and through him. "No man hath seen God at any time," says the author of the Fourth Gospel; "the only begotten Son, who is in the bosom of the Father, he hath declared him." To most of us God remains an abstraction until we see him in terms of personality.

It is in Jesus, the Incarnate Son, that we find our fullest revelation of God. But all the saints reveal him in some measure. The most striking fact to me, as I turn the pages of the Old Testament, is not the crudeness of some of its stories, but the clearness with which some of these ancient saints saw God. Here, for instance, is a psalm written centuries before Jesus was born. It begins like this: "The Lord is my shepherd; I shall not want." Our Lord found in this psalm such an accurate description of himself that he seems to say, "This poet was looking into my face as he sang his song. I am the Good Shepherd who giveth his life for his sheep." It is wonderful that certain great souls of the long ago saw God so clearly that they were able to be, in some fashion, a revelation of him to their fellows.

Samuel was a man of this type. He became in his own day a veritable way of the Lord along which God could walk to manifest himself to his people. Men saw something of God in him. Nor is his story by any means unique. The chances are that all of us had our first glimpse of the beauty of the Lord by looking into the face of some one of his saints. Listen to this exquisite confession of faith and love: "Intreat me not to leave thee, or to return from following after thee: for whither thou goest, I will go; and where thou lodgest, I will lodge: thy people shall be may people, and thy God my God." How had Ruth come to choose the God of Naomi for her own? She did so because she had seen the beauty of the Lord in the face of the woman she loved. This, I take it, is the highest service that one soul can render to another—to bring to that soul a sure sense of God.

III

The Lord appeared again. He appeared, not in the splendors of his glory, but he appeared through Samuel. Why did he choose Samuel?

Let us face the fact at once that this choice was not a matter of favoritism. We are not all of equal ability. God gives to one two talents, and to another, one. These talents are gifts. Therefore they reflect credit upon the Giver, not upon the receiver. No man deserves credit merely for receiving a gift. If you have a beautiful face, you have not yourself to thank for its beauty. Your beauty is a gift. You deserve no more credit for being handsome than your neighbor for being homely. Samuel was vastly gifted, but the Lord did not reveal himself to and through him for that reason.

Why then, I repeat, did God reveal himself to and through Samuel? It was because there was that in Samuel which made such a revelation possible. God is infinitely eager to reveal himself to every human soul. But some of us make that revelation impossible. We refuse to see. How did Samuel make it possible? We can find an adequate explanation by a glance at Samuel's background.

1. Samuel had the privilege of being cradled in the arms of a saintly mother. For years Hannah was a wife without a child. She felt bitterly the disappointment of it. Though a favorite wife, she longed for the hug of baby arms and the kiss of baby lips. In her eagerness for motherhood she turned to God in earnest prayer. God heard her. Then one day the sweet angel of suffering came, and she held a baby in her arms. She named him Samuel, "God-asked," because he was given in answer to prayer. She said, "For this child I prayed; and the Lord hath given me my petition which I asked of him."

Having received her child from God, she believed that he was still God's child. She believed that God could do more for him and through him than she herself could do. There are some mothers and fathers who are afraid to trust their children altogether with God. Hannah was not. She not only declared that God had heard her prayer and granted her request, but she added, "Therefore also I have lent him to the Lord; as long as he liveth he shall be lent to the Lord." She dedicated her son to God. Not only so, but she dedicated him in his young and tender years.

Having thus dedicated him to her Lord, she took him to the sanctuary and put him in the care of the best man she knew, the pious priest Eli. This saintly old man was far from perfect. He had made a tragic failure in the rearing of his own sons. He had two boys who were in the priesthood, but they were a curse rather than a blessing. They too might have been revelations of God to men, but they missed their chance. Their failure was the fault of their father as well as of themselves. Eli, so far as the record goes, had never done a positive wrong, but he had failed to do the aggressive right. His supreme failure was in a weak refusal to discipline his own sons. The first message from the Lord that Samuel had to deliver was one of doom for his pious old teacher and for his sons.

Listen to these words: "I have told him that I will judge his house for ever for the iniquity which he knoweth; because his sons made themselves vile, and he restrained them not." What a word that is for today when family discipline seems to many ridiculous, stupid, and antiquated! Yet a lack of discipline cheats the child of his happiness in the here and now. No child is happy whose will is never crossed. Not only so, but it is likely to rob him of his future. I am not now discussing how we should discipline our children. But what I am saying is that it would be better for the child never to be born than not to be trained. It was for lack of training that the sons of Eli, who might have been revelations of God, came to make religion detestable because of the ugliness of their own personal lives.

But though Eli made a failure with his own sons, he

rendered a great service to his day and to all the subsequent centuries through his training of this gifted youth, Samuel. One night, the author tells us, this winsome lad had a personal call from God. Up to this time his faith had been only an inherited faith. His religion had been a religion of hearsay. But now it became a religion of experience. God called Samuel, but the lad interpreted that call as a human voice. He thought it was only the call of Eli. His is a common blunder. There were those about Jesus who sought to explain the voice of God by saying, "It thundered." At other times we interpret as divine a voice that is of the earth, earthy. Blessed is the youth who has some wise saint to interpret to him the voice of God. This ancient teacher told the lad how he might be sure of God.

"Go, lie down again," he directed, "and when you hear the voice, say, 'Speak, Lord, for thy servant heareth.'" This is a direction that is just as fresh and pertinent today as it was those long centuries ago. Eli is only saying what another said in different words: "In all thy ways acknowledge him, and he shall direct thy paths." It is as we are willing to do his will that we come to know. This is the road along which any man can walk to religious certainty. Here is a word out of the experience of one of the greatest of the saints: "I know whom I have believed, and am persuaded that he is able to keep that which I have committed unto him against that day." "I believed," writes Paul, "I committed, I know." Samuel took that road and came to know. They spoke of him in later years as the seer. He was a man who had come to see God.

IV

Look next at the services that this man who saw God rendered to his needy people.

1. During the prime of his manhood he served as a judge in Israel. His position was one of power. He was a virtual king. Under his leadership Israel found a new unity and a new freedom. As a judge he visited his people, hearing their disputes and helping them to settle their difficulties. This he did so wisely and well that no man could pick a flaw in his administration.

But, in spite of this fact, there came a day when the people demanded a change. By this time Samuel had grown old. His hair was white. He was not quite so fit physically as he had once been. Then his sons had proved a disappointment. Further, the people wanted a king in order to be like the nations round about them. They wanted a king because they thought a king would be more theatrical and dramatic. Up to this time their government had been a theocracy, but now they wanted a monarchy. They were eager for God's representatives to be more showy, to make a greater appeal to the eye. When religion has lost its inwardness, men generally seek to make up for that loss by an outward display.

When these people whom Samuel had served so faithfully began to clamor for a change, the prophet naturally did not hear their demands with gladness. He did not wish to retire. He was not ready to superannuate. Being a man of prayer, he took the matter to the Lord. He was convinced that he was concerned only for the honor of God, but part of his concern was for himself. It is terribly easy to mistake our selfishness and wounded pride for the zeal of the Lord. God told his disappointed prophet that the people, in making their demands, were not so much rejecting the prophet as rejecting their Lord. He also told his servant to comply with their request. Thus was Samuel superannuated.

2. Then came the second, and really great, era in his

life. This ungrateful treatment might have embittered a lesser man. I knew a preacher some years ago who was superannuated against his will. He became so embittered over it that he alienated his own children from the church to which he had given his life. That Samuel was tempted to wash his hands of the whole business is evident from these words: "God forbid that I should sin against the Lord in ceasing to pray for you." He would never have said that if he had not been tempted to say, "All right, you do not want my services. Therefore I will not force them upon you. You have made your own bed, now you can lie on it." Samuel's Christlike magnanimity showed itself in two very definite ways.

First, in his attitude toward Saul. This young man had taken Samuel's place of rulership. The prophet could not fail to see that, though he was a giant physically, he was little better than a dwarf spiritually. How easy it would have been for him to have criticized his successor and to have made it hard for him. Instead, he became his lifelong friend. When news came that Saul had departed from the Lord, it broke Samuel's heart. He cried unto the Lord all night for this backslidden king. The next morning he paid him a pastoral visit and did his best to win him back to God. Though Saul did not listen to Samuel, he believed in him as he believed in no other man.

This is evidenced by what he did in the most tragic hour of his disappointing life. When he was near the end of his journey and his doom was closing in upon him, he felt desperately the need of help that no man could give. But, having forsaken God, he knew not where to turn. At last he decided to consult a medium. Man is incurably religious. If he does not have a real religion, then he will have one that is spurious. Do not laugh at Saul's conduct as an old folk story. There are thousands of intelligent people who are following in his steps this very day. When this medium asked Saul whom he wished to consult, he said, "Bring me up Samuel." He believed in this good man in life; he believed in him in death. He never doubted his friendship, though Samuel had to pronounce his doom.

In the second place, Samuel showed his greatness in that he continued to love and to serve his people. He did not look back to his enchanted yesterday and condemn the colorless today by comparison. Instead, he became so interested in the present and the future that he forgot all the slights of the past. *Life Begins at Forty* is the name of a book written some time ago. Indeed it does! It begins at fifty, sixty, even at seventy. It begins at any age that a man is willing to be shaken out of his comfortable rut and to do the task that is suited to his hands.

This wise prophet became peculiarly interested in the youth of his day. There are few surer signs that one has grown old and sour on the inside than his wholesale condemnation of youth. Because of his keen interest in youth, Samuel ceased to speak only the language of the generation into which he was born. He began also to speak the language of those of another generation. He found young men hungry for God, but too ignorant to know how to find him and how to interpret him to others. For these he established divinity schools. All the theological seminaries that have been built since that far-off day had, in a sense, their beginning here. He found a group of young men who were nothing more than howling dervishes, and changed them into prophets of the Lord. Thus this man through whom God came back rendered his largest service after he had been superannuated.

Here, then, is a bracing word for all of us. God is the

same yesterday, today, and forever. God is always seeking to reveal himself to man. He can reveal himself through the faith of a little child. He can reveal himself through the men and women who are in the stern stresses of the middle passage. He can reveal himself especially through those who have grown old and wise in his fellowship. So it was with Samuel. Therefore we are not surprised to read, "Samuel died; and all Israel . . . lamented him." Humble men and women in the most distant villages and the most obscure countrysides shed unaccustomed tears at the news of his death. For his home-going left "a lonesome place against the sky." This was the case because, as long as he lived, he brought to all who knew him a bracing sense of God. May this be the beautiful vocation of everyone reading these words!

A GLIMPSE OF THE AFTERLIFE

LUKE 16:19-31

While so much is being said about the afterlife, so much that is false, so much that is misleading and bewildering, it seems to me altogether wise to learn something of what is said by him who speaks with authority. The story that I have read to you fell from the lips of Jesus Christ our Lord. It was uttered by him "who came from God and who went to God." It is altogether wise to remember this. Philosophers, scholars, and wise men may speculate, and do speculate, about what lies beyond the grave. Our Lord does not speculate—he knows. He is equally at home in the realm of the seen and the unseen. He is as familiar with the yonder as he is with the here and now.

For this reason we have a right to come to this story with confidence. We have a right to come to it with reverent expectation. It was uttered by him who of old laid the foundations of the world, by him who was in the beginning with God, and who is God. Its teachings are the teachings of him in whom "dwelt all the fulness of the God-head bodily." If there is that in the story which seems to you absurd, remember that it is the utterance of eternal wisdom. If there is that in the story which seems to you heartless and cruel, bear in mind that it is the cruelty of him who loved us well enough to hang on the nails for our redemption.

As I speak to you about this wonderful story, then, I shall speak with conviction. I shall feel no fear that the ground on which I stand will have a hollow ring as I tread upon it. For I have this confidence in my Lord: he is too wise to be mistaken and too honest to deceive us. When he had the last conversation with his disciples on this side of the grave, he said to them, "Let not your heart be troubled. In my Father's house are many mansions. If it were not so I would have told you." That is, "I would not allow you to believe what is false, even though it was a comfortable belief. I would not allow you to rest your heads upon falsehood, even though it might be as soft as pillows of down. I tell you that there is a homeland of the soul. I say this, not because it meets the deepest yearnings of your heart, but because it is really true." So in the story that we have before us we may expect to find that about the afterlife which is really true.

Look now at the story. It is really a wonderful drama in three scenes. The first scene reveals a typical day in the lives of two men.

"There was a certain rich man that was clothed in purple and fine linen, and fared sumptuously every day. And there was a beggar named Lazarus that was laid at his gate, full of sores, and desiring to be fed with the crumbs that fell from the rich man's table; moreover the dogs came and licked his sores."

This, then, is the picture upon which the Master lifts the curtain. He makes us see these two individuals. He shows us how they live. He compels us to look at the rich man and also to look at the beggar. That is all. He utters no word of comment upon the character of either man.

Here is the scene: a lovely palace. You enter the palace through a magnificent portal. The halls are lined with "marble white and black, like the mingling of night and morning." The rooms are hung with the finest of tapestries.

61

And the rugs upon the floor are the choicest product of the oriental loom. There are courts of rare beauty where fountains spray from silver faucets and make lovely and listless music.

Today there is a big banquet at the palace. The select Four Hundred are being entertained. The host receives graciously. He is the best-dressed man of the company. He is cultured, refined, elegant, rich. The guests whom he welcomes are likewise elegant and refined and rich.

The scene is altogether pleasing but for one thing. There is one blot upon its beauty. There is one ugly scar upon its loveliness. At the outer gate of this palatial home there lies a bundle of dirty rags. As we look we see the rags stir a bit. It is a sick beggar that is within them trying to make himself comfortable upon the cobblestones. He too seems to be receiving today. But his guests are not refined and cultured. They are the wild, unfriended dogs of the street. These sit about him on their haunches and lick his sores. They too are starved and friendless, but withal they seem less friendless than the sick man whom they are attending.

You will notice at once that Christ has no word of condemnation for the rich man because he is rich or because he feeds well or because he wears fine clothes. Nor is there any attempt on his part to put a halo upon the beggar's head because of his poverty and rags and sickness. He simply puts the scene before us. We are forced to look at these two men. Physically they are close together. In point of circumstance they are far apart. The one is sick; the other is well. The one is rich; the other is poor. The one fares sumptuously every day; the other feeds on crumbs. The one has friends, and the other is unfriended. And as we look we realize that the tragedy of the picture is that the two never actually come together.

"There was a certain rich man"—what is the meaning of the word? Rich man—it stands for power, capacity, ability to serve. "And there was a beggar that lay at his gate full of sores"—that means need. And so we have here ability to serve and a need of service brought close together. The poor man was at the rich man's gate. That means that this poor man was the rich man's responsibility. He was the rich man's opportunity. I do not know what responsibility lay at the gate of the man across the street, but the responsibility of this rich man is very plain. The call for help is loud and insistent. Here was his chance. Here was his opportunity. Here was the safety vault in which he might have made a deposit for eternity.

But the rich man seems never to have seen the man at his gate. He was too busy with his affairs. He was too much occupied with his own pleasures, the pleasures of getting and the pleasures of spending. Not that he was unkind to the beggar—he did not have him stoned, he did not have him thrown into prison. He was not a cruel man, this rich man. At least, he was not aggressively cruel. I daresay he was better than the average. Otherwise he would have driven the old beggar away and not even allowed him to gather up the crumbs. At least the sin of the man was not that he did anything of harm to the beggar. It was rather in the fact that he let him alone.

The second scene is one familiar enough in our world. The rich man allowed the beggar to receive only the scraps, only the crumbs. Now, men cannot be saved by crumbs. God will never save the world through the mere crumbs of our time and of our energy and of our money. The beggar got only the crumbs, so quite naturally it came to pass that the beggar died.

"Ah," you say, "there is nothing startling about that."

"I have been expecting him to die for a long time," one said. Another said, "He is out of his misery, better off. To have given him bread would have been a calamity, as it might have caused him to suffer only the longer." Yes, the beggar died and nobody thought of being startled by it. Nobody thought of weeping over it. It was not at all disturbing even to the rich man, though if he had been faithful to his duty the beggar might have lived. Thousands die morally every year because we who are rich in resources, material and spiritual, are too self-centered to meet their needs.

"The rich man also died"—now, that is startling. We could easily spare the beggar, but a leading citizen that gave banquets—that is different. "The rich man also died" —he died in spite of his riches. He died in spite of his palace. He died in spite of his fine linen. One day ill-mannered Death walked in with his boots muddy with the clay of new-made graves and pushed this self-centered, feasting man out into his tomb.

The rich man died and had a funeral. The funeral of the beggar is not mentioned. Doubtless he had none. His old, sore body was found in the street and carted away with the day's garbage:

> Rattle his bones over the stones,
> He's only a beggar whom nobody owns.

But the rich man was buried. And here Christ drops the curtain.

When the curtain rises again it rises upon the world unseen.

"It came to pass that the beggar died and was carried by the angels into Abraham's bosom."

That is, he was carried into the paradise of God.

"The rich man also died and was buried; and in Hades he lifted up his eyes, being in torment, and seeth Abraham afar off and Lazarus in his bosom."

How naturally Christ passes from the seen into the unseen. With what absolute at-homeness he shows us these two men as they are in the afterlife!

What are some of the facts that he tells us through this story? What light does he throw upon the mystery of the unseen? They are facts familiar enough to Bible readers. They have been pointed out many times before. First, he tells us very clearly and unmistakably that the dead are still alive, that the man who has passed into the unseen is not asleep. He is consciously and vividly alive. This is true of Lazarus; this is true also of Dives.

And this fact of the conscious, vivid life of those who have passed into the hereafter is not taught in this parable alone. Over and over again this same truth is either implied or clearly stated. In speaking of Abraham, Isaac, and Jacob, saints who had passed into the unseen, Jesus did not count them as dead. In fact, he clearly declared quite the contrary. "For God," says he, "is not the God of the dead, but of the living."

When Jesus was hanging on the cross one of the men at his side prayed this marvelous prayer: "Lord, remember me when thou comest into thy kingdom." And Jesus replied to that prayer by giving the dying robber this promise: "Today shalt thou be with me in paradise." What did the promise mean? It means that Jesus and the dying robber were going to meet in the paradise of God that very day; that they were going to be consciously alive and conscious of each other. So death is not a sleep. All men are consciously alive beyond the grave.

The second fact we learn from this story is that these men are not only alive, but they are conscious of being themselves. Lazarus is still Lazarus. Dives is still Dives. The rich man still speaks of himself and says, "I." He is conscious of the fact that he is the same man on the further side of the grave that he was on this side. He is conscious of the same human relationships. He is conscious of the fact that he is the same individual who once knew Lazarus in this world, and who was also a member of a family of six brothers.

At death we are going to lose something, each of us. We are going to lose the physical. We are going to lose our possessions. Whatever may be our material wealth in this world, we may depend upon it that the hands of the dead are not clutching hands. Our shrouds will have no pockets. Death will rob us of all that is material.

But there is one something that death cannot take away from us. It cannot rob us of ourselves. Yesterday I was myself. I will be myself still tomorrow. I will continue to be myself as long as heaven is heaven, as long as God is God.

Of course, by saying that I will forever be myself I do not mean for a moment that I will forever possess this body that I possess tonight or this brain that I possess tonight. But this body is not myself. We are all aware of that. This body is a possession of mine. I own it. I control its movements. I can make it act in accordance with my will. I speak through its lips. I minister through its hands. I look out from its open windows called eyes and receive messages through its open portals called ears. I own a body tonight. However, it is not the same body I once owned. I am fond of change. I get a new suit of clothes for this body now and then. I also get a new suit for this soul of mine at least once every seven years. So I have already worn out five bodies and thrown them away like a cast-off garment. Yet I am still conscious of being the same self that I was in the first body I ever owned.

And, of course, it is not saying anything new to say that my brain is not myself. I possess a brain, but this brain does not control me. I control it. I have power to educate it. I have power to direct its energy. I have power to focus its thinking upon a certain object. I am in the possession of a brain, but I do not possess the same brain I once had. Neither do you. We wear out brains just as we wear out bodies. It is really amazing how some of us wear our brains out using them as little as we do, but we wear them out nonetheless. And I have had at least five different sets of brains, and yet I am still the same individual that I was when I was in possession of the first brain I ever had.

Now, if I can throw away five different bodies and five different brains and still be the same man, I can throw away this body and brain into the grave at the end of the day and still be the same. The truth of the matter is, death is not going to touch me personally at all. It is not going to touch the real "me." For this reason I am going to be exactly the same man the first minute after death as I was the last minute before death. It would work no great moral change in me to pass from one side of the Potomac River to the other, nor would it work any great change for me to pass from one side of the narrow river called death to the other.

In spite of this fact, however, there is a tremendously great tendency to believe that death will work a moral change, that you can lie down one moment self-centered, sin-conquered, godless—and, by the mere act of dying, wake up the next moment holy, sinless, and Christlike. It is absolutely false. If Christ does not save you in the here and now, do not expect death to accomplish what he was unable to accomplish. If the blood of Jesus Christ cannot cleanse you from all sin, do not be so mad as to expect that cleansing at the hands of the undertaker, the shroud, and the coffin. Believe me, that as death finds you, so you will be the instant after when you open your eyes in the world unseen.

The third fact Christ teaches us in this story is that man is not only alive and conscious of self beyond the grave, but that he remembers. Lazarus remembered Dives, and Dives remembered Lazarus. They remembered their former experiences. Dives remembered the life he used to live. He remembered his selfishness and his sin. He remembered his lost opportunities. He remembered the five brothers in the home from whence he had come, and how his own life had helped them to be selfish and godless like himself. In the afterlife you are going to remember. Memory is going to be a power that will help to intensify the joys of heaven. It will also help to embitter the pangs of hell.

Finally, Christ makes it plain to us in this story that all men are not going to have the same destiny in the world unseen. He teaches us that there is going to be a separation there between the good and the bad, between the Christlike and the Christless. These two men in the world unseen were separated. Between them, we are told, there was a great gulf fixed. Who separated them? God, you say? I deny it. They separated themselves. The chasm between Dives and Lazarus was made in this life. They made different choices here. Those different choices led to different characters. They became morally separated by a chasm as wide as right from wrong, as night from day. And that separation continued beyond the grave.

Why was Lazarus carried by the angels into Abraham's

bosom? It was not because in this life he was unfortunate. It was not because he was friendless and attended in his last illness only by dogs. It was not because he was sick and sore and neglected. He was carried into heaven because, in spite of all these calamities, he made choice of God. His name signifies "God is my help." And it was this right choice that made him a right character. And this right character made for a glorious spiritual destiny.

Dives, on the other hand, was not lost simply because he was rich. He was not cast out because he wore fine clothes and had sumptuous feasts. Dives was ruined by a wrong choice. Listen to the story. He is asking for a drop of water to cool his parching tongue. And the reply he receives is this: "Remember that thou in thy lifetime receivedst thy good things, likewise Lazarus evil things."

What does it mean? This: "Remember that in your lifetime you made a deliberate choice of the things that are seen. You deliberately chose to live for self. You turned your back upon God, and, turning your back upon God, you turned it upon your own brother. You chose to live for the gratification of your own pleasure." That is what brought ruin to Dives—not the fact that he was rich, not the fact that he lived well, but the fact that he deliberately chose to ignore God and to live for self.

Not only did Dives choose to live for himself, but he chose it in the face of the light. He knew better. He knew the life that he ought to live. When he is refused the drop of water, he asks that Lazarus be sent to his five brothers to warn them, thus implying that he was not rightly warned, that if he had had proper warning he himself would never have made the fatal choice that he did make and achieved the fatal destiny that he had achieved. But the reply to this is very emphatic and very clear. "You had," he is told, "what your brothers have—Moses and the prophets. That is light enough. And if a man will not hear them, if a man will not be persuaded by them, neither will he be persuaded though one rose from the dead."

Men are accustomed to flatter themselves with the belief that they would change their lives and become Christians if certain positive proofs of the life to come were brought to them. But Christ tells us that men are not convinced by ghosts. Men are not led to repentance by ouija boards and seances. I have known quite a number who claim to have received messages from the dead. I have never known one single one who has been made a New Testament type of Christian by such messages. God's only method of reaching men is through the truth believed in and obeyed, and if men will not hear that, they will not be saved, even though one rises from the dead.

Thus it came to pass that Lazarus found himself in Abraham's bosom. It is a Hebrew way of saying that he was in the paradise of God. He was in a place of comfort. He was in a place of joy. Dives, on the other hand, was in a place of conscious pain. While Lazarus was comforted Dives was tormented. Why was this true? It was not because God loved the one and did not love the other. It was not because God desired to save one and did not desire to save the other. Their different destinies were the inevitable outcome, I repeat, of their different characters, as their different characters were the outcome of their different choices.

The truth of the matter is that God has no way of getting any man into heaven when he has hell in his own heart. You cannot mix the living and the dead even in this life. A little child was last week carried out of a home where it was the idol, and buried. The reason for this conduct on the part of the father and mother was not because they no longer loved the child. They buried the child in spite of their love for it, because it was dead. And hell, whatever else it may be, is the burying ground of dead souls, souls that are dead in trespasses and in sin.

So the conclusion of the whole matter is this: Forever you are going to live. Forever you are going to be yourself. You are going to have to keep house with yourself for all eternity. Forever you are going to remember. Forever you are going to enjoy or suffer the destiny that you make for yourself while in this life. If it sounds foolish, remember it is the foolishness of him "who spake as never man spake." If it seems heartless, remember that it is the heartlessness of Infinite Love. Remember, too, that though some men are lost, no man needs to be lost. Every man can be saved if he will. This minute you can be saved if you will only be wise enough and brave enough to make a right choice. "Him that cometh unto me I will in no wise cast out." Will you come? Will you come now?

THE HEROIC HIGHWAYMAN

*And he said unto Jesus, Lord, remember me
when thou comest into thy kingdom.*

LUKE 23:42

You will find the text of the evening in Luke, twenty-
third chapter and forty-second verse: "Lord, remember me
when thou comest into thy kingdom." The man who
prayed this prayer was a highway robber. He was a "knight
of the road." Even now, he is dying the death of a rebel
and of a murderer, and yet I believe you will agree with
me that this highwayman is no ordinary man. I believe
when you take into consideration the circumstances under
which he prayed this prayer, you will be convinced that
he is one of the most daring thinkers and one of the most
heroic men of whom history gives us an account.

Look at the situation. It is a holiday in Jerusalem some
nineteen centuries ago. Great out-of-town multitudes
throng the streets of the city. Rome is going to execute
three prisoners today. She has chosen this day because she
desires the largest number of spectators possible. She will
let her subjects see what it means to rebel. In this way she
will make rebellion tremble and hide its face even in the
most distant parts of the empire.

And the crowd is hideously eager to witness this bloody
show. Men have always liked the gruesome. I suppose in
a measure they always will. Even today we like to see things
that are dangerous. We like to watch people flirt with death.

If there is a daring auto race, if there is an especially dangerous feat to be performed in an airship—multitudes will gather to see. We are still blood brothers of those who used to watch the gladiators fight in the arena years ago. We are still kin to those who witness the bullfight of the Spanish countries to this day. We love things that are bloody, gruesome, horrible.

The crowd is the more eager to see this show because the three men who are to die are well known. Two of them are highwaymen. They were men who had begun possibly by being zealous patriots, but, being unable to gather an army and fight in the open, they had banded themselves together into a robber clan. They had homed in the fastnesses of the mountains and had preyed upon the passersby as ruthlessly as they felt that Rome had preyed upon themselves. They were not unpopular men, I daresay. On the contrary, they were possibly thoroughly popular. They were looked upon as heroes. Had they not dared all to plague and to vex the common enemy, Rome? We are not entirely successful in holding back our admiration from men of the Jesse James type in our own day, though he had far less excuse for going upon the road than did these men.

The other man who is to die has come into prominence in an altogether different way. He has preached in their synagogues, taught in their temple. He has touched lepers into purity. He has opened blinded eyes and raised the dead. He has shown himself a religious leader and teacher of marvelous power. For this reason some have loved him with a love stronger than death. For this reason also, others have hated him with a hatred that will not endure his being on the earth.

As the procession moves out from the Roman praetorium down the narrow streets, there is much more in the appearance of the robbers to appeal to the vulgar crowd than in the appearance of Jesus. The robbers walk jauntily forward under the weight of their wooden crosses, for they are "lithe and sinewy and hard as nails." They seem unafraid. Like men they have fought. Like men they are determined to die. The other man seems almost utterly spent. His cross is more than he can bear. He has just passed through a horrible night. He has been crowned with thorns and his back has been hideously gashed by the Roman scourge. He has lost much blood and is weak, so weak that before the end of the journey another has to carry his cross.

Arrived upon a weird, skull-shaped hill outside the city gates, the four soldiers in charge of each prisoner perform the work of execution. The victims are stripped bare. A vessel of highly medicated wine is passed among them. This wine is to deaden the pain. For even in that iron age when the heart of the world was far from being tender, this poor boon was not denied even to the worst of criminals. The robbers drink, but Jesus refuses. He will meet death fully awake.

Then the victims are stretched prone upon the cross, spikes are driven into palms and insteps, and the crosses are dropped into the holes that have been digged for them. There is a spray of blood, the tearing of flesh, the straining of tendons—and then these three trees so lately planted stand laden with their fruit of infinite pain.

The soldiers now make themselves as comfortable as possible at the foot of the cross and begin dice throwing and drinking. For death by crucifixion is such a slow-footed monster that they must needs amuse themselves while their victims die.

Now it is that the jeers and the scorn and the revilings

of the crowd break out in their most blasphemous intensity. I can well imagine that the robbers, to whom little of it was directed, would have replied in kind. They had nothing to fear. Rome had already done its worst. They had reached the end of the trail. But, to the amazement of at least one of these robbers, the one who is the butt of the bitterest mockings does not reply at all except to throw round the shoulders of those who are murdering him "the sheltering folds of this protecting prayer": "God, forgive them, for they know not what they do."

Now, a scene that will soften one man will often harden another. Two men attend the same service and hear the same sermon. One man has his heart broken by it. Under the spell of it he finds his way to the cross. The other is only made the more hard, the more stubborn, the more bitter and indifferent. This was the case with these two robbers. The attitude of Jesus seems to have maddened the lesser robber beyond endurance. I think he would like to have hit Jesus in the face. As it was, he railed at him.

But on the greater robber the impression was exactly the opposite. As he had watched Jesus on his way to the cross and upon the cross, he had become convinced that he was an innocent man. He had been impressed by his perfection. So deep and genuine is this impression that the howls of the mob and the taunts of the churchmen and the revilings of his companion are becoming almost unbearable. They pain him, I think, more than the nails upon which he hangs. At last he can contain himself no longer, but, turning as best he can to his companion, he says, "Dost thou not fear God, seeing thou art in the same condemnation? And we indeed justly, for we receive the due reward of our crimes. But this man has done nothing amiss."

Look at the insight of it, and the daring. Rome has

declared Jesus guilty. The religious leaders of his day have declared him guilty. The mob has declared him guilty. Graybeards of the church are even now declaring him guilty. But these jeers and howls and false sentences cannot disguise from this discerning man the truth. There steals into his heart an absolute conviction of the snow-whiteness of this man who is dying at his side.

Then you will notice that that happened which always happens when a man comes to realize the presence of Jesus. When this robber had realized the spotlessness of the man at his side, he became conscious at once of his own spottedness, of his own guilt, of the stains upon his own soul. Against that white background he sees himself in all his moral ugliness. And he cries, as he endures the very pangs of hell, "Justly, justly. I am suffering, but I deserve every pang that I suffer. I am guilty. Against thee, thee only have I sinned and done this even in thy sight."

This man is on the way to victory. He dares face his own sin. Now, he might have taken another course. He might have nodded his head at his companion over there and said, "I am a sinner, it's true, but I am no worse than that man. He has been my companion in crime." He might have pointed out distinguished churchmen in the crowd and have said, "I am a saint beside that old hypocrite yonder with soul mummified and heart utterly dead." But men never get far in that way. It is only as we face our own sin and hate it and forsake it that we find salvation.

One of the dangers of this day is a lost sense of sin. We have lost our sense of sin because we have lost our sense of God. The man who sees God sees himself as one guilty and defiled. Isaiah was one of the best men of his day, but when he caught a vision of his Lord he put his lips in the dust and cried, "Unclean! unclean!" Job was a high-toned and moral man. But at the vision of his holy Lord he abhorred himself in dust and ashes.

There is no surer rebuke than the rebuke of a stainless life. Many a man who will never be convinced by our preaching might be convinced by our living. Sam Hadley met a beautiful woman of the street one night. She said, "Go home with me." He said, "No, you go with me." She went, and to her amazement he carried her and introduced her to his wife. They talked together a while. She was very restless and soon declared that she must go. Mrs. Hadley got her wrap for her, put it around her shoulders, and gathered her in her arms and kissed her. And the woman of sin sobbed, but she never left. Her heart had been broken at the revelation of her own self that had come to her in the light of this good woman's life.

This robber saw himself. He saw himself as a man in need, as a man sin-stained and hastening on to the second death. And he reached out his hand for help in this wonderful prayer: "Lord, remember me when thou comest into thy kingdom." It was not a coward's prayer. It was not the prayer of one who has insulted a million chances and who now calls on God, not because he loves goodness, but because he wants to dodge a penalty.

There are people like that. That smaller robber was on that order. He said, "If thou be the Christ, save thyself and us." He is only interested in escaping the penalty. He is only praying as you prayed when you thought you were going to die. He is only calling on God as you called on him during the storm. That sort of praying is born not of love of goodness nor love of God. It is born simply of slavish fear. It is the prayer of a coward.

But whatever else this man was, I say, he was no coward. Will you notice this: he dared take the part of Jesus before he took his own. Before he asked Jesus to help him, he did all that was in his power to help Jesus. He tried to defend him from the howling mob. He did the best that he could to put his torn and tortured body between Jesus and those who were tormenting him. Do you think that was easy?

It was not easy. When that robber did that, he put himself in a crowd absolutely by himself. He stood utterly alone. There was not another man in all the wide world that dared speak for Jesus and defend him at that moment. Every disciple has forsaken him. The women stand in the distance and sob in silence. The churchmen jeer at him. And Rome crucifies him. Only one man dares to defend him, dares to speak for him. Millions will rally to him in other years, I know, but let us honor this man who dared befriend his Lord when all others had forsaken him. Let us honor the courage and devotion of him who uttered the last kindly and tender words that ever gladdened the ear of the dying Son of God on this side of the grave.

Then look at the faith of this man. He calls Jesus Lord. Did ever a man exercise such marvelous faith? Some of you have never called him Lord, in spite of the fact that he has come to you as the Christ who has been the molder of history. You have never called him Lord though you were reared in a Christian home. You have never called him Lord, though you had a godly father and a praying mother. This man called him Lord.

He called him Lord in the most trying of all possible circumstances. Peter called him Lord when he had witnessed his miraculous power in the draught of fishes. Thomas called him Lord when he had shown him the hands that had throttled death and hell and the grave. Paul called him Lord when he had seen him risen with a resplendent glory that had smitten him blind. But this man called him Lord when to the crowd he seemed even less lordly than the reviling robber by whom he hung.

There was a sign above his head: "Jesus, the King of the Jews." That was the joke of the day. Nothing was matter for deeper scorn and derision than that word. This dying man a king! But to this clear-eyed robber the superscription was no fiction. He saw in this man the King Eternal. Hear him: "Lord, remember me when thou comest into thy kingdom." How sure he is of his kingship! He doesn't say, "Remember me *if* thou comest." We might at least have expected him to put it that way if he had considered him a king at all. But his faith goes far beyond that. He said, *"When* thou comest." Not "If you happen to outride this storm, remember me," but "I know, Lord, that your victory is sure. So when you come into your kingdom remember this poor robber who hung with you on the nails."

Was ever a faith so wonderful? There is the King and he has no throne but a cross. He has no crown but the thorn marks. He has no scepter save the nails that pinion his hands. He has no retinue but a jeering and howling mob. His whole royal wardrobe is in the hands of the Roman crapshooters. And yet this man penetrates the disguise of nakedness and the disguise of shame, and even the dusky disguise of death itself, and sees in him the King Eternal, whose head is to be crowned with many crowns.

Notice, too, that he believes this King is able to grant favors beyond death. He believes that this dying Lord is the very Lord of life. Think of it—this robber is dying. He knows it. He is fisticuffing now with the last grim enemy. The man at his side is dying more rapidly than himself. He knows that, too. Yet dying robber unto dying Christ speaks of life. And in the gloaming of the night of death he lays plans with him for eternity. I tell you the faith that sent martyrs to the stake, the faith that removes mountains into the depths of the sea, is but child's play in comparison with the faith of this man.

"Lord, remember me"—mark you that he does not ask for a throne. He does not ask, as the sons of Zebedee, for a place on his right hand or his left. He somehow feels that one thought of this dying man will be enough for him for time and for eternity. And so he says, "Lord, remember me."

Did Christ hear that heroic prayer? Did he listen to this dying man who appealed to him in the hour of his sorest agony? Yes. He heard him. He heard him and gave to him an answer. And there is no sweeter word that ever fell from his lips: "Verily I say unto thee, today thou shalt be with me in paradise."

We would be much poorer in every way if we did not have this word. Hear what a marvelous light it throws upon the immediacy of salvation. How long does it take Christ to save a man? How long does it take him to snap his fetters and break his chains? How long does it take Jesus to make the worst of men clean and unspotted in his sight? How much time is required before this sinful human heart of mine can become a sharer in the divine nature? Answer: It may be done instantly. In the quickness of the lightning's flash I may be reborn. I may this instant become a new creature in Christ Jesus.

Some people laugh at instantaneous conversion. They want to save the world by a process of evolution; but evolution would have been a poor remedy for this dying man. He needs salvation now. And that is just the salvation that Christ had and has to offer. "Now is the accepted time and today is the day of salvation." "Today shalt thou be with me," he says. And that was his birthday. And this may be yours, however far in sin you may have gone. Today you may be with Jesus. Tonight you may leave this church in the sweetness of his fellowship.

This answer of our Lord also throws a flood of light upon the ground upon which we may hope to meet Jesus in peace by and by. "Today shalt thou be with me in paradise." Why? For the simple reason that this dying robber has begun by being with Jesus in the here and now. He has just claimed a present salvation; therefore it is perfectly reasonable for him to expect a future salvation. He has come to know Jesus personally here; therefore he has sure grounds for hoping to meet him and know him yonder.

And there is no other sure basis of hope. Do not, I beg you, expect salvation at the hands of the cemetery. Do not hope for redemption through the power of the coffin and the shroud. There is one, and only one, who saves—"There is none other name under heaven given among men whereby we must be saved." And if this Jesus cannot save you in the here and now, then he cannot save you at all. But if he can and does save you now, he can and will save you forevermore.

"Today shalt thou be with me in paradise"—where is that? I do not know. What is it? It is the abode of Jesus and those who have trusted in him. I take it it is heaven. And he makes this place very sure to us. He asserts upon his very oath that this dying robber is going to be with him in paradise. Then there is a heaven. There is a place where love shall find its own. There is a land where God shall take us upon his great mother lap and wipe away all tears from our eyes.

"Thou shalt be with me"—this man had become a sharer

in the nature of Christ. As best he could, he had shared in his shame, and now he is going to share in his glory. He is going immediately. He is going today. He is with Christ now. He will be with him forevermore.

"Who shall separate us from the love of Christ? Shall tribulation, or distress, or persecution, or famine, or nakedness, or peril, or sword?

"Nay, in all these things we are more than conquerors through him that loved us.

"For I am persuaded that neither death, nor life, nor angels, nor principalities, nor powers, nor things present, nor things to come,

"Nor height, nor depth, nor any other creature, shall be able to separate us from the love of God, which is in Christ Jesus our Lord."

Therefore I beg you to lay hold on Jesus tonight, that you may claim him for your Savior now and forevermore.

A WINSOME INVITATION

Come unto me.

MATTHEW 11:28

My business with you in these words is very simple. I am not here as an entertainer, though what I have to say should be vastly interesting. I am not here primarily as a teacher, though my message should be instructive. I am not here to lay upon you any kind of external compulsion. I am here as the bearer of an invitation. The invitation is not mine, but Another's. My sole business is to deliver it as plainly and as winsomely as I can. It is up to you to decide whether this invitation is addressed to you personally or not.

When I was a boy, one of the big hours of the day was when the mail reached our village. Those fortunate enough to be present gathered around the little corner that was boxed off in the racket store to hear the postmaster call the mail. He called each piece just as one might call the roll. When we heard our names, we answered and received our letter, or postcard, or catalogue, or sample copy of the *Home Comfort,* as the case might be. Naturally, there was no compulsion about this. The postmaster did not put a gun in our faces and compel us to take the bit of mail that was rightfully ours. We could take it or leave it at our own choice. He had discharged his duty by calling our names and making our mail available.

I

Now, my position is akin to that of the postmaster. I am here to call the mail. If you find this invitation addressed to you, it is your privilege to accept it. If you find that it has nothing whatever to do with you, then, of course, you have the right to be indifferent and to let it alone. Listen, then, to the invitation; and see if it calls your name. "Come unto me, all ye that labor and are heavy laden, and I will give you rest. Take my yoke upon you, and learn of me; for I am meek and lowly in heart: and ye shall find rest unto your souls. For my yoke is easy, and my burden is light." This invitation is extended to two groups, to two types of individuals.

1. Jesus is here inviting the laborers: "Come unto me, all ye that labor." The word "labor" implies more than work. Work is a privilege. It is a source of great joy. Nobody can be happy who is not in some sense a worker. Work is also a wonderful safeguard against temptation. The hours of our greatest peril are always our hours of idleness. Then, work is a great healer of hurt hearts. How many have forgotten in some measure their sore wounds by hard and diligent work! But labor means work that is carried on at the price of weariness and pain. It is work that is so heavy and hard, or so futile, that it becomes an agony. It is work that has degenerated into toil, the toil of the treadmill, the toil of monotonous struggle that ends in lean achievement or in utter frustration.

One day, for instance, Jesus commanded his disciples to enter into a ship and to go before him to the other side of the lake. They obeyed with all eagerness. For a while their little vessel glided in romantic beauty over the silvery water. But suddenly a tempest swept down upon them. The sea was whipped into a rage. The angry winds pounded them; and, row as they might, they could make no progress. The work of the beginning was now changed into toil. They were straining far harder than when the sea was calm, but they were getting nowhere. Strain as they might, all they got out of it was weariness, blistered palms, frustration, and defeat.

Possibly some of you feel yourselves in this class. You have taken life seriously. You have tried hard to be and to do your best. But your efforts seem to have brought you little or nothing. The whole struggle has resulted mainly in vanity and vexation of spirit. A woman came to my study some time ago, glared at me in desperate fashion, and said, "I feel like I want to hurt somebody. I would like to hurt you." Then, after a pause, she went on, "I have tried to be a Christian. I have worked hard in the church. I have tried to make a Christian out of my son, but he is not a Christian. He is a criminal. That is all my efforts have come to, and I am going to quit. I tell you that right now, I am never going to come to church again. I am never going to pray again." Poor broken and defeated thing! Hers is an extreme case, I know. But perchance some of you can sympathize with her. If life for you has become a task too hard to manage, if you are carrying on with an effort that has in it a bit of agony, the agony of a too bitter struggle or of defeat, then yours is one of the names that Jesus is calling.

2. The second group that is invited is the burdened: "Come unto me, all ye that are weary and heavy laden." If you have come to God's house struggling under a weighty load, then this invitation is meant for you. This is the case regardless of what that load may be. Your burden may not be like that of the man at your side; it may not be like that of the minister; but the chances are that most of us here present are conscious of carrying some kind of burden.

Yours may be a burden of anxiety. You may be tormented

by fear. You look to tomorrow and turn hot and cold with fright. Maybe you fear for yourself. Your income is uncertain. Your position is insecure. Your health is failing. Pain is walking with fire-shod feet along every nerve of your body. Or maybe you fear for another who is dearer to you than your own life. Maybe that one is slipping into an untimely grave. Worse still, maybe sin has taken him captive and is robbing him of all moral and spiritual beauty. Yours may be a burden of fear.

Then, you may be struggling under a burden of sorrow and disappointment. You once dreamed great dreams, but they have come to nothing. You have traveled a road that promised to lead to great and worthwhile adventure, but it has led to a quagmire or to a desert. Perhaps death has slipped into your family circle and has taken one who was so dear that life has seemed empty since he has gone. Perhaps you have been robbed by an enemy even worse than death. Anyway, you have become acquainted with tears; and you are here, bearing your burden of sorrow.

There are others whose burden is that of self-will. Without any desire to hurt themselves or anybody else, these have been bent on freedom. They have determined to live their own lives. But the experiment has proved vastly disappointing. In the *Arabian Nights* a gentleman, out of sheer kindness, took a feeble old man on his shoulders to give him a lift; but, once there, the old man refused to dismount. He was the Old Man of the Sea, and he became a crushing weight upon the shoulders of the one that had sought to befriend him. But self-will is a burden even heavier than the Old Man of the Sea. All toilers, then, and all burden-bearers are included in this invitation. I have an idea that includes about all of us.

II

What does Jesus invite us to do? His invitation is twofold.

1. He says, "Come unto me." This is an invitation that careless handling has left a bit tarnished. Familiarity has, in some cases, bred contempt. It is possible to say, "Come to Jesus," in such a fashion as to repel rather than to woo and to win. But we must not allow its careless handling to rob us of its deep and enriching meaning. There are some ultramoderns who even laugh at this winsome word; but, in spite of that, it is unspeakably rich to all who will give it a hearing.

This is a word that was on the lips of Jesus again and again. He could never see a crowd without holding his hands out to them, as a mother might hold hers to a tired and frightened child, and saying, "Come to me." He meant something when he said it. He means something still. He means that we can come. We can do so instantly, in the twinkling of an eye. This is an invitation to us to accept his lordship, to enlist in his service, to become his disciples. "Come unto me, all ye that labor and are heavy laden." Every man of us may accept that invitation, here and now, if we will.

2. But not only does he say, "Come unto me," but "Take my yoke." This word is capable of two interpretations. It may mean "Accept the yoke that I give; submit to my authority." But perhaps the better interpretation is this: "Take the yoke that I bear." The one, "Come unto me," calls for a single act of decision; the other, "Take my yoke," for a dedicated life. Jesus himself bore a yoke. He invites you and me, and all the toilworn and the burdened, to accept the yoke that he himself bears. This first word, then, "Come unto me," is an invitation to enlist. The

second, "Take my yoke," is an invitation to share in the campaign.

What was the yoke of Jesus? It was the yoke of complete surrender to the will of God. The life of Jesus was a dedicated life. He lived every day and every hour within the will of God. He emphasizes this fact over and over again: "He that hath sent me is with me: the Father hath not left me alone; because I do always those things that please him." "I came down from heaven, not to do mine own will, but the will of him that sent me." When he was sitting by the well-curb and his disciples were urging him to eat, he replied, "My meat is to do the will of him that sent me, and to finish his work." Then, when he stood at the end of the journey and his earthly life lay behind him, he faced his Father with these words: "I have glorified thee on the earth: I have finished the work which thou gavest me to do." We are invited, then, to come to Jesus and to take upon ourselves the yoke that he bears.

III

Then, our Lord gives us certain reasons for accepting this invitation. He will not undertake to force his yoke upon us. Whether we come and accept his yoke or not is purely optional. He has too great a respect for personality to undertake to force us. He could not if he would. He would not if he could. He will never compel any man to come to him. He will not compel any man to bear his yoke. All he will ever do is invite. Whether we accept or not is up to us.

But though it is our privilege either to accept or to reject the yoke of Jesus, it is not our privilege to reject all yokes. The most that is offered us is a choice of yokes. If we refuse his yoke, then we must in the nature of things bear some yoke. "Choose ye this day whom ye will serve," said a warrior of the long ago. By this he meant that we are going to serve somebody or something. We can choose the service of Christ if we will. But if we refuse his yoke, another yoke, that of self or sin, will be forced upon us. Every man must bear some kind of yoke. It is optional whether we bear the yoke of Jesus or not. But having refused his yoke, the bearing of another yoke is not optional. Some yoke, I repeat, we must bear whether we wish it or not.

Why, then, are we to bear the yoke of Jesus? The reason given by the Master is a bit surprising. It is not what we should have expected. He does not urge us to bear his yoke because by so doing we may make our way to heaven. That is no doubt the case. The bearing of his yoke will certainly do this for us. But that is not the reason offered by our Lord. No more does he urge his yoke upon us because the bearing of it will lead to our highest usefulness. This is also the case. But that is not the reason that he gives.

Why, then, I repeat, does he urge his yoke upon us? For this strange reason: "My yoke is easy," (or "kindly," as Moffatt translates it) "and my burden is light." Jesus is here speaking out of his own experience. Having worn the yoke of a dedicated life, he commends that yoke to us. "I have found the bearing of this yoke easy and kindly," he says. How strange! Why, the bearing of it cost him everything. It made of his life one long self-giving. It caused him to be a Man of Sorrows and acquainted with grief. It meant for him the tragedy of Gethsemane and Calvary and Joseph's grave. It led him to that exceeding bitter cry, "My God, my God, why hast thou forsaken me?" But, in spite of all this, he declares that his yoke is easy.

Not only does he make this claim, but his whole life

bears out the truth of it. If his life was one long crucifixion, it was still the most radiantly joyful that was ever
lived on this planet. In his last prayer with his friends, he
makes this request for them: "that the joy that is mine
may be theirs." In spite of the fact that he is under the
shadow of the cross, he has a present joy that is so bound-
lessly rich that he longs that those he loves may possess it.
Then he has a peace that knows no bounds. That too he be-
queaths to his friends as he goes away: "Peace I leave with
you, my peace I give unto you." Speaking out of his own
rich experience, he says to all of us, "My yoke is easy. My
yoke is kindly."

IV

Why is this the case?

1. The yoke of Jesus is kindly because the bearing of
it brings us rest. The rest here spoken of is not the rest
of idleness. That is not in the strictest sense rest at all.
While conducting a funeral recently, I noticed that the cas-
ket had upon it these words: "At rest." But I must confess
that they made no great appeal to me. I have never been
quite so weary as to long for that kind of rest. The rest
that Jesus offers is not rest from the yoke, but rest under the
yoke. It is a rest that is born of right relations, that results
naturally from rightness with God, rightness with ourselves,
and rightness with our fellows. It is a rest that will keep
work from becoming the agony of toil. When perfect, it
will enable us to "work for an age at a sitting and never be
tired at all."

2. His yoke is easy because it is borne from a great
motive. The lightest task may be sheer drudgery if we have
no high reason for the doing of it. But the heaviest task

becomes sheer poetry if done from a great motive. Jesus found his yoke easy because he cared. He had a burning passion for God, and a burning passion for men. Therefore, it was a joy to serve them. "For the joy that was set before him," the joy of helping, he "endured the cross, despising the shame." Love always delights to serve. The only time that love's heart breaks is when it can no longer serve.

Some years ago the sweet angel of relief came to an afflicted boy near my home in Tennessee. That boy had been for years a great sufferer and a constant care, especially to his mother. Sometimes she would sit and hold him in her arms all the long night through. Therefore, when death touched him into peace, some said, "Of course, his mother will grieve, but what a relief!" But this is what she said to her minister: "My little boy has·gone, and I cannot get to do anything for him any more." She had borne a heavy yoke, but it was easy because it was borne from a great motive.

3. Then, the yoke of Jesus is easy because it fits. More than one team of oxen had been driven before the little shop where Jesus worked to have a new yoke fitted. The carpenter saw how the old yoke had wounded their necks until the drawing of the lightest load was painful. What was the matter? The yoke did not fit. Jesus saw to it that the yoke he made would never wound, because it was a perfect fit.

Some of us are suffering from sore wounds, wounds of the conscience and wounds of the heart. What is the matter? We have been wearing a yoke that does not fit. There is no surer road to wretchedness than that. A brilliant graduate in one of our leading universities took his life a few years ago. He left a letter that was a literary gem. In giving his reason for his rash deed, he said, "I have grown so utterly tired of doing as I please that I long to bathe my weary soul in the ether of eternity." Why had he become so weary? It was not the weight of his yoke. His weariness rather was born of the fact that his yoke did not fit. That ill-fitting yoke made him so wretched that he could not bear to live. Only one yoke fits us; that is the yoke of Jesus.

4. Finally, his yoke is easy, as another has pointed out, because it is one that is shared. In Ian Maclaren's beautiful story "His Mother's Sermon," the mother makes this appeal to her son: "If Christ offers you his cross, you will accept it, because he always carries the heavy end himself." That is true. When he offers us his yoke, he carries the heavy end. Not only so, but that yoke becomes a bond of union between him and us. It becomes a medium through which his amazing power and helpfulness are transmitted to ourselves. Sharing the yoke with him, we shout with Paul, "I can do all things through Christ which strengtheneth me."

This, then, is the invitation that I am sent to deliver. Bear in mind that it is not mine, but his whose I am and whom I am seeking to serve. Therefore, it is my earnest hope and prayer that you may be able to look past the minister into the face of him who gives this invitation and who pledges himself to make good its every promise. He is standing in our midst at this moment, holding out his hands to us, and saying what he said to burdened, weary, and flustered souls in the long ago: "Come unto me, all ye that labor and are heavy laden, and I will give you rest. Take my yoke upon you, and learn of me; for I am meek and lowly in heart: and ye shall find rest unto your souls. For my yoke is easy, and my burden is light." This is his winsome appeal to all of us. What response have you made? What response will you make today?

GOD'S ENDLESS QUEST

The eyes of the Lord run to and fro through-
out the whole earth, to show himself strong
in the behalf of them whose heart is perfect
toward him.

II CHRONICLES 16:9

What a bracing and winsome word this is! The book
of Second Chronicles is a rather prosaic book, but here
it breaks into exquisite poetry. Here is a gospel as fresh
and appealing as that of the New Testament. This word
thrills and heartens us because of the light that it flashes
upon the face of our Lord. It shows him as the eternal
seeker after man. But it heartens us no less because of
what it tells us of ourselves. If it lights up for us the face
of God, it sheds an equally revealing light upon the face
of man. It tells us something that we are prone to forget;
and that is that, in spite of all his follies, faults, and sins,
man is a grand creature. He has that in him, I know, which
makes him akin to the beasts; but he also has that which
makes him close akin to God.

I

If you are, for the moment, in a spirit of pessimism,
if you feel disposed to say something disparaging about
man, then you can let yourself go without any great fear of
overstating your case. You can agree with the cynic who
declared that he could believe in humanity if it were not

for folks. You can snarl with Carlyle that the world, as well as England, is made up of so many millions, mainly fools. In fact, there is no ugly word that you cannot say about man, and speak sober truth. There is no trust that he has not betrayed. There is no crime that he has not committed. There is no depth of moral infamy that he has not sounded. At his worst, he seems indeed a very son of the devil.

But if you feel inclined to take an optimistic view, you can do that and be just as correct as the pessimist. For if there is nothing too bad to say about man, it is equally true that there is nothing too good to say about him. There is no danger that he has not dared. There are no heights that he has not undertaken to scale. There is no costly sacrifice that he has not been glad to make. He has crossed all seas, penetrated all forests, left his consecrated ashes upon all shores. If there is much of clay in him, there is also much of fine gold. If he is a son of Adam, he is also a son of God.

One mark of man's greatness is that he is possessed of an insatiable hunger for God. Other creatures are content so long as their physical needs are met. But this is not the case with man. When the Prodigal had spent his all and was sent into the field to feed the swine, he and the swine had something in common. They both had to eat. But when the swine had eaten their husks, they were satisfied. They could then lie down in perfect content. But, for the Prodigal, this was impossible. He was haunted by home voices and home memories. "Lord," sang an ancient poet, "Thou hast been our dwelling place." God is the heart's true home, and we are forever homesick so long as we are away from him. This hunger and thirst after God is universal. It belongs to the best of men. It belongs also to the worst. The chief difference between the best and the worst, in this respect, is that the best know that it is God after whom they are hungering, and the worst often do not. Here is a psalmist who is wise enough to know what is lacking in his life. He knows the one way to satisfaction for himself. Therefore, he sings, "As the hart panteth after the water brooks, so panteth my soul after thee, O God."

But there are others who are less wise. They realize that there is something lacking. They know that they have hungers and thirsts that have never been met. But often they try to meet their needs by wilder parties, or by accumulation of more things, or by grasping some poor second-best. I saw a caged eagle the other day. There is always something vastly pathetic about a caged eagle. This great bird sat with his burnished brown wings folded slovenly about him. He did not even seem to care that he had wings. He looked out upon the world with lackluster eyes. Had I said to him, "What is the matter with you?" perhaps he could not have answered. Maybe he did not know. But I knew. He was missing the role that he was meant to play. He was not made for a cage. He was made for the sky-land and the upper air. He was made "to bathe his plumage in the thunder's home." Even so we are made for God, and we can never find rest or peace without him. This is a mark of our greatness.

But the supreme mark of our greatness is not our hunger for God, but God's hunger for us. If we cannot get on without him, neither can God get on without us. Man's quest for God has been timeless and universal. But God has always sought man before man sought him. It is the realization of this truth that causes this author to sing, "The eyes of the Lord run to and fro throughout the whole earth, to show himself strong in the behalf of them whose heart is perfect toward him." We seek because we are sought. "We love him, because he first loved us."

It is this love, this endless quest of God after man, I repeat, that constitutes man's supreme claim to greatness. A few years ago, the papers were full of criticism of a certain woman named Wallis Warfield. They told how she had been twice married, and how in both instances she had divorced her husband and had wrecked her home. Many regarded her as a rather cheap and chaffy woman. But there was at least this argument that there was some worth about her in spite of her ugly past. There was a man that saw enough in her to uncrown himself for her, and to give up the greatest empire in the world. If Edward has any worth at all, then his love argues for something of worth in the woman for whom he gave his very all.

Now, if such a love argues for the worth of Wallis Warfield, how much more does the love of God argue for our worth. I am aware that it is not always easy to believe this. A certain psalmist as he looked out upon this amazing universe found it hard to believe in the worth of a creature so seemingly insignificant as man: "When I consider thy heavens, the work of thy fingers, the moon and the stars, which thou hast ordained; what is man, that thou art mindful of him? and the son of man, that thou visitest him?" Then the psalmist answers his own question and does it in a grand way. "Thou hast made him," he contends, "but a little lower than God." He is, therefore, a great creature. He is the one supremely worthful creature in the universe. So precious is he that, at his worst and lightest, he outweighs the world. Hence, Jesus said, "What shall it profit a man, if he shall gain the whole world, and lose his own life?" The fact that man cannot get on without God marks him as a great creature. But

the fact that God cannot get on without him is his supreme
mark of greatness.

II

Now, it is this endless quest of God after man that is
the central theme of the Bible. This quest is the central
theme of the Bible because it is the biggest fact in human
experience. There is nothing more true or more arresting
than God's endless quest for man.

We meet it on the very first page of the Book. I am
aware that we can make sorry reading of the first chapters
of Genesis if we bring to them a wooden mind. But read
aright they are as fresh as the dewdrop on the lip of a
rose. When Adam through his rebellion had broken with
God, he was restless and afraid. But, strange to say, he did
not begin at once to seek God. On the contrary, he hid
from him. Adam did not cry, "My God, where art thou?"
It was rather God who cried, "Adam, where art thou?" It
is ever so. Hiding has been characteristic of man through
the centuries. It is God who has always to begin the search.

Just as we find God searching for man on the first page
of the Bible, so we find him on its last page. Here we see
his face a little more clearly. By this time we have a somewhat better understanding of him. But he is on the same
loving quest. "And the Spirit and the bride say, Come. And
let him that heareth say, Come. And let him that is athirst
come: and whosoever will, let him take the water of life
freely." Thus, when we get our first glimpse of God upon
the pages of his Book, he is in pursuit of man. When we
get our last glimpse, he is still upon the same endless quest.
He is still holding out his arms, saying, "Come unto me."

Now, this quest that is pictured at the beginning and

the end runs throughout the entire Book. Here is a prophet speaking on God's behalf: "Ho, everyone that thirsteth, come ye to the waters, and he that hath no money; come ye, buy and eat; yea, come, buy wine and milk without money, and without price. Wherefore do ye spend money for that which is not bread? and your labor for that which satisfieth not?" And again: "Come now, and let us reason together, saith the Lord: though your sins be as scarlet, they shall be as white as snow; though they be red like crimson, they shall be as wool."

Some of you will remember "The Hound of Heaven," by Francis Thompson. He felt himself pursued by a loving God from whom there was no escape. There was a certain psalmist that had a like experience. He ran from God, even as you and I. But he was pursued by a love that would not let him go: "Whither shall I go from thy Spirit? or whither shall I flee from thy presence? If I ascend up into heaven, thou art there: if I make my bed in hell, behold, thou art there. If I take the wings of the morning, and dwell in the uttermost parts of the sea; even there shall thy hand lead me, and thy right hand shall hold me."

This record of the quest of God after man reaches its climax in the ministry of Jesus. He summed up his mission in these words: "The Son of man is come to seek and to save that which was lost." He told the story of a certain shepherd that led his flock home in the gloaming, to discover that one sheep was missing. Ninety-nine were safe, but he could not let this one silly and wayward sheep alone. He set out into the wilds and sought for that foolish creature till he found it. He then laid it upon his shoulder and brought it home. So great was his joy over his successful search that he had to give expression to it by inviting his friends and making a feast. "And God is like that," said

Jesus. "There is joy in heaven in the presence of the angels over one sinner that repenteth."

It is tremendously significant that in his quest for man there is no price that God is not willing to pay. To be convinced of this it is only necessary for us to turn our eyes once more to the cross. The death of Jesus on Calvary is a historical fact. But the cross means infinitely more than one single historic event. Jesus on the cross is God on the cross. What Jesus suffered is what God is suffering, not for a few black hours, but from eternity to eternity. The cross tells of the continuous heartache of God as he goes on his endless quest for man. Truly,

> But none of the ransomed ever knew
> How deep were the waters crossed,
> Nor how dark the night that the Lord passed through
> Ere he found his sheep that was lost.

III

If God is forever seeking man, how does he seek him? How may we know that he is out questing for us at this moment? God seeks us in a vast variety of ways. He taxes the infinite resources of his wisdom in order to find us.

1. He seeks us through our daily experiences. When you see the sun rise in the morning, God is saying, "Will you let the Sun of righteousness rise upon you with healing in his beams?" As you slake your thirst at the wells and fountains of this world, God says, "Whosoever drinketh of this water shall thirst again: but whosoever drinketh of the water that I shall give him shall never thirst; but the water that I shall give him shall be in him a well of water springing up into everlasting life." As you who are fathers and mothers seat yourself at your well-filled tables, and serve

99

the plates of your children, God says, "If ye then, being evil, know how to give good gifts unto your children, how much more shall your Father which is in heaven give good things to them that ask him?" God is speaking to us through our daily experiences, both of joy and of sorrow.

2. God speaks to us through the beautiful lives of those about us. All of us have been privileged to know at least a few who have about them a charm and winsomeness that can be accounted for only in terms of God. All of us have been privileged to know one here and there upon whose life the beauty of the Lord rests as the sunshine rests upon the hills. I saw such beauty on the face of my mother. I saw it in the strength of my father. I have seen it in other faces till I have said wistfully, "I wonder if God can do for me what he has done for my friend?" God seeks us through the Christlikeness of those about us.

3. Then, God seeks us through our own individual needs. Sometimes we feel keenly our need of cleansing; we cry as passionately as Lady Macbeth, "Out, damned spot! out, I say!" We long desperately for one who can

> Minister to a mind diseased,
> Pluck from the memory a rooted sorrow,
> Raze out the written troubles of the brain,
> And with some sweet oblivious antidote
> Cleanse the stuff'd bosom of that perilous matter
> Which weighs upon the heart.

God is seeking some of us through our conscious need of forgiveness.

Then, God is seeking others through a sense of frustration and defeat. "My inner resources have all broken down," said a desperate man to me the other day. "I have sworn off drink times without number, yet I know that as soon as I leave you I'm going to get drunk." It is not so bad with you, perhaps; yet you are depressed by a sense of failure. The good you vowed to do you fumbled; the evil from which you turned in horror gripped you. Today you feel like wailing with Paul, "O wretched man that I am! who shall deliver me?" God is calling you and me through our sense of personal need.

4. Finally, God is calling us through the needs of others. We are living through desperate days. It is my conviction that every one of us would like to do something to help. But how powerless we are! We remind ourselves of that embarrassed host of whom Jesus told: "Which of you shall have a friend, and shall go unto him at midnight, and say unto him, Friend, lend me three loaves; for a friend of mine in his journey is come to me, and I have nothing to set before him?" There you have the whole tragic truth— "I have nothing to set before him." This host has a guest that is hungry. But when he goes to his larder, he finds it as empty as the cupboard of Old Mother Hubbard. Such is too often our experience. There is not one of us that is not confronted by calls for help, by opportunities to serve, that in our own strength we simply cannot meet.

When this host found himself in this embarrassing position, he was deeply troubled. It is easy to see the marks of care upon his face. Then, his face lights up and his heart bounds with joy. What is the cause? He has thought of his friend. He is not in such a bad plight after all. Therefore, he hurries away through the night to knock in confidence on the door of that friend. Nor does he knock in vain. By and by, he is home again. But he does not return empty-handed. Just how many loaves he has we do not know. But of this we may be sure: he has as many as he needs.

I wonder if you and I will be thus wise? We too are

being asked for bread that we cannot give. We are face to face with doors to which we find no key. If the demands made upon us are too great for our strength, what are we to do? Remember that you too have a Friend. Through the needs of others that you long to meet, he is calling. It is the testimony of those who have tried him that he is able to change our painful inadequacy into an amazing adequacy: "He is able to make all grace abound toward you, that ye, always having all sufficiency in all things, may abound to every good work." The man who wrote that is speaking out of his own experience. In fact, he declares with a kind of joyous swagger, "In Christ who strengtheneth me I am able for anything." It is such ability that we need. God is calling to us through our consciousness of that need.

IV

Why does God thus seek for man?

He is not doing so in order to cheat him. He is not trying to compel him to lead a life that is lean and mean. It ought not to be necessary to say this, yet it seems that it is. This is the case because so many of us are still a bit supicious of God. We are still afraid of him. We are afraid that if we give ourselves wholly to him, he will ask too much of us, and thus take the blue out of our skies and the lilt of joy out of our songs.

There is a word in the book of Genesis that says, "My Spirit shall not always strive with man." God's Spirit does strive with us, but what is the meaning of this striving? It means that we resist God. It means that God is trying to get us to make one choice, when we are determined to make another. It means that God is seeking to induce us to take the upper road, when we are bent on taking the lower. It means that God is inviting us to receive the best, when we are insisting on the worst or upon a poor second best. If there is strife in your home, it means that the inmates of that home do not agree. If there is strife between you and God, it means that you are working at cross-purposes with him. The most tragic fact in the world is this quarrel of man with God.

Why, I repeat, is God seeking us? He is doing so because he is so eager to help. "The thief cometh not, but for to steal, and to kill, and to destroy: I am come that they might have life, and that they might have it more abundantly." This God of infinite love wants to show himself strong on our behalf. He is eager to make us strong to stand upon our feet, victorious over self and sin. He wants to make us strong in the service of others. If he fails to do this, it will be our fault, not his. Whenever he has an opportunity, he does show himself strong in behalf of those whose hearts are perfect toward him.

But what does it mean to have a perfect heart? It does not mean one that is sinless. It means one that is consecrated, dedicated. All God is asking of you and me is ourselves: "Behold, I stand at the door, and knock: if any man hear my voice, and open the door, I will come in." This quest of God is endless. He sought you yesterday. Before your mother's lips kissed you, he was there. He has been seeking you through all the changing years. It is a fact of today. He stands even now at your door. Perchance he will be there tomorrow. But he is surely there today. He will not break the door down. But if you open it, he will come in; and his coming will give you an adequacy for the business of living.

A little more than half a century ago a yacht landed one evening at the wharf of Inverness, Scotland. Two young men disembarked and set out upon a walking tour. They got lost. Late that night they knocked at the door of a farmer's cottage; but though they pled that they were both hungry and cold, the farmer kept the door shut in their faces. They went to another cottage a mile or more away. This farmer was more hospitable. Though it was past the midnight hour, he opened his door. To his surprise he found that one of the young men desiring to get into his humble home was a prince who later became beloved George V of England. What must have been the shame and humiliation of his neighbor when he found that all unwittingly he had shut the door in the face of his king. It is your King that is knocking at your door. It is your King that is seeking for you: "The eyes of the Lord run to and fro throughout the whole earth, to show himself strong in the behalf of them whose heart is perfect toward him." He will show himself strong in our behalf if we are trustful enough to give him a chance.

WHAT HAPPENED AT PENTECOST

What meaneth this?

ACTS 2:12

Pentecost is the greatest event in the history of the Christian church. But, in spite of this, I am persuaded that for many earnest people it has little or no meaning. Some have become so mystified by that about it which is passing and nonessential that they have missed what is essential and abiding. Therefore, instead of fixing our minds upon the events of this story that we confessedly do not understand, let us think of that about it which we cannot help but understand. Let us forget for the moment the fiery tongues and the rushing wind and think of the change that this experience, whatever its nature, wrought in the disciples themselves. Having considered what this experience did for these friends of Jesus, we may be the better able to judge what that experience was.

I

What, then, did Pentecost do for the disciples themselves?

1. It welded them into a brotherhood. Any close reading of the Gospels will reveal the fact that one chief purpose of Jesus was to build a brotherhood. "By this," he said, "shall all men know that ye are my disciples, if ye have love one to another." He recognized that there were two

types of personalities in the world—one made for hate, the other for love. One works toward the dividing of men, the other toward the uniting of them. He claimed that he himself was a uniting force. He claimed further that all who were engaged with him in the building of men into a brotherhood were his friends, and that all others were his enemies: "He that is not with me is against me; and he that gathereth not with me scattereth abroad." His purpose, therefore, was the building of a brotherhood.

But, in spite of the fact that Jesus gave his energies wholeheartedly to this high task, at the time of his death he seems to have made but little progress. He had gathered about him an inner circle of twelve men. But while these were outwardly one, inwardly they were far from being united. It is at once distressing and depressing to realize that they went into their last meal with their Master, spitting hot words at each other as they wrangled over the old question as to who should be greatest in the kingdom. It was the Master himself who had to assume the role of a slave and wash his disciples' feet. Not one of them was brotherly enough to undertake this lowly task. But for Pentecost, this little organization would doubtless have melted like a rope of sand.

But after this experience in the upper room, Doctor Luke could say, "The multitude of them that believed were of one heart and of one soul." This oneness belonged to the original group that had been friends of Jesus before his crucifixion. Into it had been brought orthodox Jews of the homeland. Into it had also been brought foreign-born Jews from whom those of the homeland had been separated by a wide chasm. Into this brotherhood came a little later despised Samaritans and Gentiles. Thus men and women of different races and nationalities, of widely different social standing, were brought together in the bonds of a common brotherhood.

So close were these ties that those who had once been far apart worshiped and took communion together. Not only so, but at first they shared their material substance: "Neither said any of them that aught of the things that he possessed was his own; but they had all things common." This is the nearest approach to Christian communism that we find in the New Testament. It was a communism of spending, not of earning. As to detail it was imperfect. But the spirit that prompted it was an altogether right spirit. It was a spirit of brotherliness.

It was this devotion of one Christian to another, this spirit of brotherliness, that was one of the most impressive characteristics of the early church. The pagan world looked on these little "colonies of heaven" with wistful wonder. "How these Christians love each other!" they said in amazement. And, because they wanted to love and be loved, they were drawn into these little groups. To this day there is nothing quite so impressive as a church that is a brotherhood. It is equally true that there is nothing that more grossly misrepresents our Lord than a church that is torn by strife and discord. Let the membership of any church get to fighting among themselves, and the devil may take a holiday so far as that church is concerned. Pentecost welded the friends of Jesus into a brotherhood.

2. Then, through this experience, these disciples became literally obsessed by a passion for witnessing. They had an irresistible urge to share their experience with their fellows. No sooner had the multitude come together saying, "What meaneth this?" than Simon Peter was ready with an answer. He stood up with the eleven, Luke tells us. There was one spokesman, but every member of the

group bore his testimony by standing up with the spokesman. One weakness of much of our modern witnessing is that so often the present-day Simon must stand up without the eleven. Those that should be there to back his testimony, to give it pungency and power, are not present. Simon Peter, with the backing of his fellow saints, so testified that men were cut to the heart, and some three thousand were brought into the church.

A few days later Simon Peter, with John, is on his way to prayer meeting. At the gate of the temple, he is met by a professional beggar. This man asks for alms. Neither Peter nor John has any money, but they do have a passion to share their experience. Therefore, Simon preaches to this professional panhandler with the same hot enthusiasm that he has preached to the vast multitude. Not only so, but he preaches effectively. There is a new face at prayer meeting that day. This beggar is changed into a giver. He enters with Simon and John into the temple, "walking, and leaping, and praising God."

Other days have passed, and these two apostles have clashed with the authorities and are under arrest. These authorities are a bit at a loss to know what to do with them. But at last one offers this happy suggestion: "Let us straitly threaten them, that they speak henceforth to no man in this name." Therefore, they call Simon Peter and John and command them "not to speak at all nor teach in the name of Jesus." But Peter and John answer and say, "Whether it be right in the sight of God to hearken unto you more than unto God, judge ye. For we cannot but speak the things which we have seen and heard." Silence, they maintain, is for them an utter impossibility. They can no more cease from speaking than the grass can cease from growing green at the kiss of the springtime.

That these disciples were speaking only sober truth is evidenced by the rebuke of the authorities when they are again put under arrest. Listen to what they say. These authorities seem full of righteous indignation. "We commanded you not to teach nor to speak at all in the name of Jesus, and you have filled all Jerusalem with your teaching." How amazing! Among those that had heard the message were foreign-born Jews who were visiting in Jerusalem. One of them was a brilliant young chap by the name of Stephen. He at once came to be possessed by the same passion for telling his story. He witnessed with such power that his hearers, unable to resist his words with logic, resorted to stones. In fact, they dragged him outside the city and mobbed him.

Then what happened? It was now evident that to witness was dangerous. They could not do so except at the risk of personal danger. "Therefore," the story continues with strangest logic, "they that were scattered abroad went everywhere preaching the word." Thus, when these authorities sought to put out the holy fire that Pentecost had kindled, they failed utterly. Instead of putting it out, they only scattered it. Thus, by and by, the whole Roman world was set on fire. This was done, not by preaching from the pulpit, but by the testimony of nameless nobodies who laid almost violent hands on every chance passerby to tell him of the amazing happenings that had taken place in their own lives and in those of their fellows. Pentecost gave to the friends of Jesus a passion for witnessing.

3. This experience also gave to the disciples an incredible joy and hopefulness and courage that fill us with wistful wonder to this hour. The very first impression they made

upon outsiders was that theirs was the joy of the intoxicated. "They are full of new wine" was the easy explanation. Most of us know how a mild form of intoxication banishes the gloom, changes sadness into gladness, timidity into courage, and want into wealth. There is a classic Tennessee story of a poverty-stricken brother who met a friend that was on the point of moving to Texas. "I have a brother in Texas," he informed his friend. "I want you to tell him for me that my crops have failed, my hogs have died. Unless he helps me, I don't see how I can get through the winter." But a boon companion immensely cheered this impoverished man from his flask. Therefore, when he again met his friend an hour or so later, he merely said, "I have a brother in Texas. If you see him, tell him that if he needs anything just to let me know."

This absurd joyousness seems to have been born, at least in part, of the mad certainty of these disciples that they were sure to win. They believed that the kingdoms of this world were actually going to become the kingdoms of our Lord and of his Christ. In this mad faith, they faced stark impossibilities with holy laughter. They encountered the most deadly dangers unafraid. Opposed, arrested, publicly whipped, they knew neither discouragement nor resentment. They, rather, rejoiced that they were counted worthy to suffer shame for the sake of their victorious Lord. Thus, they lived in joyous expectancy. They were possessed by a boundless optimism and a dauntless courage that were all but irresistible.

4. Finally, this experience brought to these disciples amazing power. In fact, it enabled them to do what any sane man would have said was flatly impossible. Suppose one had said to a spectator who saw that little prayer-meeting crowd of one hundred twenty on the way to the upper

room in the temple, "There moves a group that is going to shake this entire city. They are going to shake the whole Jewish nation. They are going to shake the whole Roman world. Age-old abuses like infanticide and slavery are going to vanish before them. They are going to breathe on all the subsequent centuries like a spiritual springtime." Who would have believed it? "Impossible!" any sane man would have said. Yet, history declares that this actually did hppen.

II

This, then, is the effect: a brotherly church, a church with a passion for witnessing, a church with a joyous optimism and a dauntless courage, a church with amazing power. What was the cause? How did this group of believers come to be this kind of church?

Suppose we listen to the testimony of those who were present and who participated in this great event. They explain the change that had been wrought in themselves in terms of the Divine. They use varied words to express this conviction, but it all adds up to this: they have not simply come upon new evidences of God or of the resurrection of Jesus; they have, rather, come to a new and compelling awareness of God himself. They have come to realize beyond a peradventure that the Christ who was crucified is really alive. Not only so, he is both with and within them, individually. He is also among them as a group. They know that in giving the Holy Spirit, God has given himself. Thus they tell us that the change that has been wrought in them has been wrought by God, and God alone.

It is my conviction that their testimony is true. I believe this because no other explanation will satisfy. We simply cannot account for what these ordinary men and women became and what they did in any other way. Then, I believe that their explanation is correct because it really does explain. They became the kind of men and women, and did the kind of work, that I should expect God-possessed men and women to become and to do. After this experience they ceased to imitate Christ painstakingly and came to reproduce him spontaneously. They sing with St. Paul, "For me to live is Christ. . . . I am crucified with Christ: nevertheless, I live; yet not I, but Christ liveth in me." Should I say, "Tennyson liveth in me," you would expect me to sing in some fashion as Tennyson sang. These people, claiming to be indwelt of Christ, went out to live even as he lived.

Look, for instance, at this picture. Here is a man, brilliant, gifted, possessed by that love of life that belongs to young manhood at its best. Yet, this young man, Stephen by name, meets an untimely death. Because he dares to speak his deepest convictions, he is dragged without the city gates and cruelly mobbed. But he dies without bitterness, and there is a light upon his face that was never seen on land or sea. As he falls asleep, he prays this prayer: "Lord, lay not this sin to their charge." That marks him as a close kinsman to him who, when hung on the cross, prayed thus for his enemies: "Father, forgive them; for they know not what they do." We cannot account for such lives except in terms of God.

Just as we cannot account for what these men became apart from God, no more can we account for what they accomplished. They were without social standing. They were without wealth. They did not have enough influence to avoid the whipping post and the jail, the arena and the stake. Yet they turned the world upside down. But they never think of these mighty changes as wrought by themselves. "Do not look on us," Simon Peter warns, "as if by our own power or holiness we had done this. God has thus glorified his Servant Jesus." And always, when Paul reports the results of his missionary efforts, it is not what he and his fellows have accomplished, but what God has done through them. They could no more have accomplished what they did accomplish apart from this experience of God than a drop of water could change the Sahara Desert into a flower garden. This is the only explanation that really explains.

III

What, then, does Pentecost mean for us?

It means that this same transforming and empowering experience of God is for you and me. This is the testimony of Simon Peter as he spoke on that distant day: "The promise is unto you, and to your children, and to all that are afar off, even as many as the Lord our God shall call." This is to be the experience, not of the exceptional Christian, but of all Christians. It is an experience that is perfectly normal. Any other is subnormal. Nothing is more evident than that our Lord never intended that you and I should carry on in the energy of the flesh. Through our very failures, he is saying to us what he said in the long ago: "Apart from me, ye can do nothing." It is only in and through him that we can become and do our best.

It is, therefore, highly reasonable that the experience that made these early saints what they were should be available for us. Certainly there was never a greater need for a God who is able to do exceedingly abundantly above all that we can ask or think than there is today. Only God can enable us to save a civilization that threatens to collapse into an abysm of blood and tears through unbrotherly hate. If there is not a power that can remake us and equip us for the task of building the kingdom of God, then I see no hope for our world.

If, then, this experience is available for us, how can we enter upon it? How do we avail ourselves of that mighty power called electricity? We do so by discovering the laws of electricity and being obedient to them. It is thus that we avail ourselves of the power of God. "We are his witnesses of these things; and so is also the Holy Ghost whom God hath given to them that obey him." As the room is flooded with sunshine when the blinds are lifted, so our lives are flooded by his presence when we open the door for his incoming. He is not merchandise to be bought. He is a gift to be received: "Of his fullness have all we received."

On the farm where I spent my boyhood, under the deep shade of beech and oak trees, there is a great, flat rock. Upon the face of this rock, hands that have doubtless been dust for centuries once chiseled a basin. In spite of the fact that this basin is as lifeless as death, it sings and prattles with one of the most luxurious springs that a thirsty man ever kissed upon the lips. Go to this spring in the dead of winter, or in the noontide hush of midsummer, and you will find it prattling and laughing like a happy child. How is it that this basin offers its life-giving cup to every passerby through all the changing years? In answer to this question, the basin can only point to the majestic hill that towers in the background, and say, "Of its fullness have I received." It is such receiving that makes the finest of giving possible for ourselves. "If any man thirst, let him come unto me, and drink. He that believeth on me, as the scripture hath said, out of his inner life shall flow rivers of living water. (But this spake he of the Spirit, which they that believe on him should receive.) "

THE VICTORY

The victory is ours, thank God!

I CORINTHIANS 15:57 (MOFFATT)

Here is a word that thrills with the deathless joys of Easter. It speaks home to our deepest longings, and to our highest and holiest hopes. It is a word to make us stand up and cheer. The man who gladdens us with this heartening declaration has the victory of which he speaks looking out from his own eyes and ringing in his own voice. He looks upon hard-pressed men and women, like ourselves, who are but shattered fragments of broken families, and who are hurrying on to what looks like final defeat, and shouts, "We have won. It is ours to set our feet upon the neck of our foe and bound with joy and gladness. The victory is ours, thank God!"

I

What is this victory that makes Paul so joyful?

There are victories that are so temporary and trifling that to win them is of little consequence. They do not last. Often they fail to satisfy, even for the brief moment that they are ours. Then there are victories that mean something to a very few, but to the many they mean nothing at all.

For instance, a few days ago our newspapers carried the name of a young chap who had been the most intimate friend of my son while we were living in Birmingham. This deserving young fellow, who is as poor as a church mouse, had entered a movie contest. He had written some fifty words on why he liked *You Can't Take It with You.* By so doing, he won a prize of ten thousand dollars. The victory was his. Of course, it brought him great gladness. His friends also naturally rejoiced with him. But these were comparatively few. To the many his victory simply meant nothing at all. But this victory over which Paul is shouting means something to all of us.

Almost a quarter of a century ago the Allies won a war. What a shout of joy went up with the signing of the Armistice! "The victory is ours," we cried, "thank God!" But what an unsatisfactory victory it has proved to be! We see now that it had in it far more of sorrow than of joy, more of war than of peace, more of death than of life. This is the case with so many of our victories. Comparatively few of us win. But even when we do, our victories are generally defective. Some are so because they concern only the few. Many of them are unsatisfactory because they are so fleeting, or have in them the seeds of defeat. But the victory over which Paul shouts is for all of us, and it abides for all time and for all eternity.

What, then, I repeat, is this victory? It is an all-inclusive victory. It includes the conquest of every foe that we are called upon to face. But the foe of which Paul is thinking especially is that most vindictive and victorious of all foes, which we call death. Paul claims that victory over death is ours. Surely this is a matter of vital interest to all of us. This is true for one reason, at least, and that is because death is an experience through which all of us must pass. This is the case regardless of what may be our attitude toward death. Our attitudes are quite varied.

Some of us, for instance, because we fear death, seek

to ignore it. We try to get rid of this unwelcome adventure by refusing to think of it. Some time ago a little chap stood in front of me, tightly closed his eyes, and said, "You can't see me." But the fact that he had shut his eyes did not put mine out. I could see him in spite of his deliberate blindness. So it is with death. We cannot get rid of this grim fact, or any other, by simply refusing to face it. The message of Easter therefore concerns us all, because all of us must pass through the experience of death.

Then there are others who try to treat death, and what lies beyond, with entire indifference. "One world at a time," they say with a shrug. "It does not matter to me in the least whether the grave ends all or whether it does not." This attitude may be possible for some of us for a little while. It may be possible as we think simply of our own dying. But it is not possible when we think of the passing of those we love. However you may feel about your own going, you cannot see your mother pass into the valley of the shadow and say, "It doesn't matter to me in the least whether she has become a clod, or whether she is consciously alive in the Father's house." You cannot say such a heartless word as you hold your own baby in your arms. Believe me, there comes a time to all of us when about the biggest question in the world is this age-old question: "If a man die, shall he live again?"

Paul is here affirming that death is not a terminus but a thoroughfare, not a blind alley but a gateway. We are going to continue to live after the experience of death. This is the case whether we desire to do so or whether we do not. In a conversation with a friend some time ago, he justified a bit of conduct that he did not think quite ethical by saying, "But a man must live."

"Certainly," I answered. "A man must live. But if by that you mean he must live a certain number of days, months, or years, here, about that I do not know, and neither do you. But somewhere, out beyond the experience of death and the grave, a man must live."

But Paul means far more in his assertion of victory than that we shall merely continue to live. The victory that thrills Paul is not the thought of continued existence, but of continued right existence. It is only this kind of victory over death that makes everlasting life worthwhile. Merely to exist is not enough. Tens of thousands fling out of life in the here and now. They find the life that now is so intolerable that they cannot stand to see it through till the whistle blows. Unless, therefore, there is a quality of life richer than the one they now possess, it would only be direst tragedy for it to continue into the eternities. But when Paul shouts, "The victory is ours," he means not simply that eternal existence is ours, but eternal right existence. This is the only victory that would not have in it more of sorrow than of joy.

II

Upon what does Paul base his conviction of victory? We may be sure that he has some reason for the faith that is in him. Paul is not a mere credulous dullard. He is one of the gigantic intellects of the centuries. Why, then, does he claim the victory?

1. One reason for his making this claim is that he believes in the resurrection of Jesus. As to his reasons for so believing, it is not my purpose to speak now. But that he did so believe, no one can deny. The resurrection of Jesus is central in Paul's preaching, as it is in the

preaching of his fellow Christians of that day. When he sums up his gospel, he does so in these words: "I delivered unto you first of all that which I also received, how that Christ died for our sins according to the scriptures; and that he was buried, and that he rose again the third day according to the scriptures." Even assuming that Paul does not claim that the resurrection of Jesus is proof positive that we shall rise, he certainly is convinced that the fact of his resurrection makes our own rising a strong and reasonable hope.

2. Then, I think Paul believes in victory over death because he believes in the supreme worth of human personality. He believes that the universe is rational. He cannot, therefore, conclude that a reasonable God will throw away the one superlative value that he has created. Personality is the one thing in this world that is of real value. When Jesus put the most chaffy personality in one pan of the scales and the world in the other, the world shot up as if it were a mere bit of thistledown. Would it not be a strange thing if a maker of fine vases were to work at his task with no saner purpose than to dash the work of his hands to pieces at the close of the day? Paul is sure that this world is not a mere madhouse, presided over by a mad God. He is sure that it is rational. Therefore he believes that the victory is ours.

3. Paul believes in victory over death because he is keen enough to realize that we are living in the unseen in the here and now. We have a silly saying, "Seeing is believing." But if we believe only in what we see, then we do not believe in any of those forces and values that are supreme. We do not believe in the law of gravity, for not one of us has seen it. We do not even believe in faith or in love. I asked a company of small boys and girls

the other day, "What is love?" They sat in utter silence, just exactly as you would if I were to ask you the same question. But not one of you would for that reason deny the existence of love. All our lives are conditioned in the here and now upon the unseen.

But you say, "I have seen people die and pass into the unseen, but I have never seen any of them come back." True; but did you see them before they went? In speaking of your friend, you say, "He has a beautiful personality." No doubt, but did you ever see that personality? Not once. You have never seen me, and I have never seen you. Of course, I have seen the house in which you live, and you have seen the house in which I live. But that is all. If you lose a finger, you have not lost the slightest bit of your personality. The same is true if you lose an arm or a limb. In fact, some of you have thrown away more than a half dozen bodies, but you are still the same personalities you were before. Therefore, if you can continue to be yourself while you throw your body away on the installment plan, it is reasonable to believe that you will go on being yourself after you throw it away in a lump sum at the close of the day.

4. But Paul's supreme reason for claiming victory is a present experience. Not only is he living now in the presence and power of the unseen, but he is living victoriously. In the fellowship of his risen Lord he is finding life a daily triumph. Of course, if life is for you a present defeat, it will not be so easy for you to believe in future victory. Sometimes we try to persuade ourselves that we can lie down in moral failure and wake up victorious. But such a faith has no encouragement in the New Testament. If God cannot give us victory here, we cannot be very sure that he can give it to us anywhere. How futile

to expect the undertaker, or the coffin, to do for us what our victorious Lord has failed to do. But since Paul is living now in the realization of victory, it is only reasonable to expect that that victory, won through Christ, will go on forever. Therefore he joyfully asks, "Who shall separate us from the love of Christ?" Then he brushes all foes aside as so many flimsy nothings as he shouts, "I am persuaded, that neither death nor life, ... nor any other creature, shall be able to separate us from the love of God, which is in Christ Jesus our Lord." Walking with the stride of a conqueror today, he believes that he will go on conquering forever.

III

What is to be the practical effect of this high faith? Suppose we should be able to join in Paul's glad shout, "The victory is ours!" what would it do for us? I am sure it would do for us something of what it did for him. What, then, did this high faith do for Paul?

1. It put a song of gratitude in his heart that absolutely nothing could hush. We find this valiant saint in all sorts of trying situations. At times, he is being stoned, whipped, imprisoned. We find him at times seemingly forsaken of God and man. But we never find him without his song of gratitude. That song here rises to thrilling heights as he sings, "The victory is ours, thank God!"

2. This faith made Paul a tireless worker. It ought to do the same for us. "Be ye steadfast, unmoveable, always abounding in the work of the Lord, forasmuch as ye know that your labour is not in vain in the Lord." "Here," he claims, "is a place where you may invest with the assurance that your investment will never go for nothing." That

ought to quicken our interest. We know what it is to suffer loss. Some of us have trusted the wrong bank. We have put our money in the wrong enterprise. But here we cannot lose. Jesus tells us that the man who gives so much as a cup of cold water in his name makes an investment for eternity. We are to work, therefore, in the assurance that those for whom we work are creatures of eternity, and that what we do for them is as abiding as God.

3. Then this fact enabled Paul to face the future—both the near future and the far future—not only with calm confidence, but with eager expectancy. A lad of fifteen, who used to attend our services, faced the fact recently that he must go early through the experience of death. There always seems something especially tragic in the passing of those who are yet in life's green spring. But this lad had been greatly blessed by having a wise and consecrated mother. Therefore he was able to face this new experience somewhat as he might have faced his first ocean voyage or his first flight in an airship. "I do not mind," he said; "there are so many things that I want to know." So it was with Paul. He looked upon his entrance into the other life as his finest and gladdest adventure.

IV

How may this victory become ours? The apostle is in no doubt as to the answer to this question. We do not win by sheer force or by grim determination. This victory is a gift. It is a gift of God through Christ. That ought not to surprise us. How did physical life become ours? Not through our own efforts. There was a mother that went down into the valley of the shadow of death for us. Our life was a physical gift from her, and primarily a gift from God. And so it is with eternal life. "Thanks be to God, which giveth us the victory through our Lord Jesus Christ."

How, then, do we get hold upon this life that means victory in the here and now, and victory forever? We do it by getting hold on God through Christ. And this we do by trusting him enough to put our lives in his keeping. "He that hath the Son hath life." "He that heareth my word, and believeth on him that sent me, hath everlasting life." "This is life eternal, that they might know thee the only true God, and Jesus Christ, whom thou hast sent." To possess Christ, therefore, and to be possessed by him, is to have a present victory. It is also to have a victory that will last forevermore. To be able to say, "I know whom I have believed," is to possess a quality of life over which death has no power.

This is far more than mere theory. So far as my experience goes, I have yet to find one living in the consciousness of God who was not sure of life both here and yonder. Years ago, I watched my father pass "to where beyond these voices there is peace." He had a good voice. He used to lead the singing in our village church. As the end drew near, he stretched out those once strong hands, that were very weak now, and sang, "Jesus, Lover of my soul, let me to thy bosom fly." He was joyously confident that the Everlasting Arms, upon which he was leaning as he pushed his tired feet into the waters of death, would sustain him through those waters, and on into the eternal yonder. Sure of God's sufficiency in the here and now, he was sure that he would prove sufficient forevermore. This is also our faith. Therefore, we join our voices with that of St. Paul, and shout, "The victory is ours, thank God!"

THE SUPREME QUESTION

Who say ye that I am?

MATTHEW 16:15

Jesus had gone with his disciples to the district of Caesarea Philippi for a brief retirement. Here he asked this inner circle of friends two questions. The first of these questions had to do with the impression that he had made upon the people during his brief ministry. "Who do men say that I am?" he asked. I daresay that Jesus already knew the answer to this question quite as well as his friends. He was therefore not so much seeking information as he was seeking to help these friends to a clear and solid affirmation of their own faith.

In answering this question his disciples did not tell the whole story. They passed over the ugly criticisms that they had heard. They said nothing of those who had accused their Master of being a winebibber and a glutton and a friend of publicans and sinners. Instead, they told him only the complimentary things that they had heard. They declared that some had been so impressed by his fiery earnestness that they thought he might be John the Baptist come back from the dead. Others had felt the rugged strength of him and had called him Elijah. Others had been gripped by his tenderness and had named him Jeremiah. Others still, feeling that he embodied the very finest qualities of the heroes of the past, said that he was one of the old prophets.

This was the very climax of the complimentary. To be likened to a living prophet might be anything but flattering. Real prophets, while they are alive, generally manage to get themselves heartily hated. But to be likened to one of the great prophets long since dead was praise indeed. Yet Jesus heard these words of high commendation without the slightest enthusiasm. I daresay he was no more thrilled by them than he is thrilled today when we see in him only a personality so great that he cut history squarely in two.

We are accustomed to honor our illustrious dead. We celebrate the anniversaries of certain select souls whose achievements in point of character and conduct have been outstanding. We write books to remind ourselves of the virtues that made these great personalities what they were and to quicken our sense of gratitude for the high service they rendered. We impress upon our children a sense of obligation and responsibility to pass on to others the lighted torches that we have received from their hands. But when life grows hard and we find ourselves in the midst of bleak winter, none of us turn to George Washington in memory of his heroic struggle at Valley Forge. As much as we honor him, we do not seek help from him. Those who think of Jesus as a great prophet are altogether right, but that is not enough. That answer aroused no enthusiasm in Jesus.

Having asked this question about other men's opinion, Jesus asked the disciples to speak for themselves. He put the question to them personally: "Who say ye that I am?"

This is a question to which we might well await the answer in breathless anticipation. Other men spoke from hearsay or from seeing Jesus once or twice. But these disciples are the star witnesses. They have been with him constantly. They have heard all his words; they have seen all his deeds. What is their answer?

When they first began to follow him, they had no clearly defined answer. They found him amazingly exciting. They found him by far the most winsome personality they had ever known. At times he shocked them. At times he thrilled them. At other times he filled them with awe and wonder. He set them whispering to each other, "What manner of man is this?" Whoever he was, they were sure that he was vastly greater than any other they had ever known.

Now the cross was only about six months away. The Master had taken them for a retreat to Caesarea Philippi. Evidently he thought that they had been with him long enough to have reached some definite conclusion. They had seen him in solitude and in the midst of crowds; they had been by when he had prayed, when he had preached, when he performed his works of wonder. So he now put to them this question: "Who say ye that I am?"

Impulsive Simon speaks up for them all. In a tremendous answer he affirms his faith: "Thou art the Christ, the Son of the living God." That is, Simon is saying, "I have found in thee the very values that I seek and that I find in God."

And what was the reaction of Jesus? Did he rebuke Simon, as any honest man who was mere man would have done? When, a few years later, Paul and Barnabas had created such enthusiasm in Lystra that the people were on the point of offering them sacrifices because they thought they were gods, what was the reaction of these good men? They were horrified. They repudiated such honor though it came very near to costing Paul his life.

But what, I repeat, was the reaction of Jesus to Simon's answer? He did not rebuke Simon. He rather pronounced a blessing upon him. With wholehearted enthusiasm he said, "Blessed art thou, Simon Bar-jona: for flesh and blood hath not revealed it unto thee, but my Father which is in heaven." He thus declared that the conviction of Simon is the truth, a truth that he had come to possess because he had been illuminated by the very light of God.

"Thou art the Christ, the Son of the living God." That was no passing notion, no spur-of-the-moment guess later seen in another light. The certainty of Simon and his fellow disciples that Jesus is God come in the flesh did not weaken with the passing of the years, but rather grew stronger. Having witnessed the death and resurrection of their Master, and having experienced Pentecost, these men became absolutely certain that the same Jesus with whom they had walked the roadways of Galilee was alive forevermore. They became certain that he was both with and within them as a living presence. Not only so, but they became the kind of men and did the kind of deeds that we should expect God-possessed men to become and to accomplish.

I

Is the faith of these disciples your faith? Today Jesus is searching our hearts with this question: "Who say ye that I am?" This is an abiding question. In every age it is the most important question with which men have to deal. It is therefore the most important question that confronts you and me today. This is not simply my conviction; it is the conviction of Jesus himself. It is so important that if we give it a wrong answer, though if it were possible we might give a right answer to every other question, life must be an adventure of failure and of tragedy. It is so important that if we give it a right answer, though if it were possible we might give a wrong answer to every other question, life would still be an adventure of joy and victory.

Listen to these daring words of Jesus: "Whosoever heareth these sayings of mine, and doeth them, I will liken him unto a wise man, which built his house upon a rock. . . . And every one that heareth these sayings of mine, and doeth them not, shall be likened unto a foolish man, which built his house upon the sand." Thus does Jesus claim to be the arbiter of human destiny. He claims that whether nations or individuals rise or fall, survive or perish, depends upon their attitude toward him.

If you remind me that Jesus is here talking about his sayings, his teachings, and not about himself, I answer that Jesus and his teachings are one. He did not claim merely to teach the truth. He said, "I am . . . the truth. . . ." He himself is Christianity. Listen to him: "Blessed are they which are persecuted for righteousness' sake. . . . Blessed are ye, when men shall revile you, and persecute you, and shall say all manner of evil against you falsely, for my sake." "For righteousness' sake" and "for my sake" are synonymous. This is the case because Jesus is the very incarnation of righteousness. He and his teachings are one.

Recently a distinguished minister declared that in order to be a Christian it is only necessary to share the faith of Jesus. This faith he summed up as faith in a fatherly God and in the brotherhood of man. He asserted that our attitude toward Jesus himself is not of prime importance. However much truth there may be in that assertion, this I can say with absolute conviction: Such is not the Christianity of the New Testament. It is not the Christianity possessed by the disciples, nor is it the Christianity taught by Jesus. The supreme question of the New Testament is not "What think ye of the faith of Jesus?" or "What think ye of Christ?" It is "Who say ye that I am?"

How flatly this contradicts the conviction held by so many today—that what one believes is a matter of no great importance! There are still intelligent churchmen who are lukewarm in their attitude toward the missionary enterprises of the church because they are possessed of a hazy belief that one faith is about as good as another. Christianity may be good for Occidentals, but it might not work so well for those living in the Orient. Yet the law of gravity works just as well for the one as for the other.

I read somewhere that a committee of Japanese waited on the philosopher Herbert Spencer years ago to discuss with him the wisdom of adopting a state religion for Japan. He thought that such a step might be wise. Then, when they asked what religion they should adopt, he agreed that their own Shintoism, being a native religion, might be quite as good for them—if not better—as any other, not excepting Christianity.

Now, had a friend told Herbert Spencer after this interview that he had assisted in placing an infernal bomb under the Japanese nation that would one day blow it to bits and leave black wounds on the rest of the world, he would have heard him in utter incredulity. This would have been the case because Spencer was an unbeliever and looked upon one faith as about as good as another.

But, regardless of what Spencer had to do with it, what actually came of the adopting of a religion on the part of Japan that taught that the emperor is divine? Multitudes took that creed seriously. Believing that they had the Son of Heaven for their emperor, they naturally came to believe that a people so highly favored were destined to rule the world. One who had lived long in Japan declared that when he would tell a Japanese friend that he did not share his faith that his nation was destined to conquer the world, this friend would not become angry; he would just be astonished that one should be so ignorant and illogical. Thus the attack on Pearl Harbor, the fanatical heroism with which the Japanese fought, were the natural outcome of their faith. What they believed wrecked them and caused them to seek to wreck the world.

The greatest threat to modern civilization today, in my opinion, is atheistical communism. What is wrong with the Communist? It is not that he by nature differs from ourselves. If you were to prick him, he would bleed. He is not made of the slime and ooze of things while we are made of far finer material. Yet here is a man who acknowledges no loyalty except that to his political party. There is no other trust that he will not betray. There is not a crime that he is not ready to commit. Why is this the case? It is because of what he believes.

What one believes, therefore, is a matter of great importance. This is the case because beliefs are creative. As a wrong faith issues in wrong character and wrong conduct, even so a right faith issues in right character and right conduct. Therefore when Jesus searches us with this question, "Who say ye that I am?" he is asking a question of supreme importance. Upon the answer we give to that question depends the destiny of the individual and the destiny of the world.

II

"Who say ye that I am?" That question is intensely personal.

Some time ago a friend of mine sent a manuscript to his publisher. It happens that this friend is a great reader. In writing his book he seems to have said to himself, "Why should I read so widely and not use what I have read?" Therefore he fairly crowded his manuscript with quotations. The result was that it was returned a few weeks later with this notation: "Too many quotations. We want to know what you think."

When Paul reached Rome as a prisoner, his fellow Jews gathered about him to hear what he had to say. "We know," they declared, "that this sect to which you belong is everywhere spoken against. You Christians have a bad reputation. But we desire to know what you think." "Evidently," they seemed to say, "something big has happened to you. Something has brought you through. Tell us what you think of the Christ whose you are and whom you serve. Who do you say that he is?"

In the same way I bring this question to your own heart and mine. Who do you say that Jesus is? I am happy in the conviction that there are those who find in him just what these early saints found. He is to many of you a "friend that sticketh closer than a brother." He is your Lord and Master, your personal Savior. You too can sing:

> Thou, O Christ, art all I want;
> More than all in thee I find.

For those of you who have not come to this bracing certainty I have this good news: You too may give a satisfying answer to this question out of your own experience. You too can say, "I know whom I have believed, and am persuaded that he is able to keep that which I have committed unto him against that day." Certainly that is a consummation devoutly to be wished.

Christianity is a religion of giving—worldly goods, time, talents, love, our very selves. But it is also a religion of receiving. When God gave himself in the person of Jesus Christ in that distant day, some refused to receive the gift. Here is one of the saddest sentences ever written: "He came unto his own, and his own received him not." But there were those who did receive him. That sad sentence is followed by one of the most thrilling ever written: "As many as received him, to them gave he power to become." That is what Jesus is constantly doing for those who receive him. He gives them the power to become. Simon received power to become a rock of Christlike character. Fanatical and narrow John received power to become an apostle of love. To all he gives power to become new creations in Christ Jesus.

Receiving him, we not only receive power to become Christlike, but we also receive power to give somewhat as he gave. There were those in that distant day who declared, "We have no king but Caesar." Built upon that foundation, their houses were swept into oblivion long centuries ago. There was a far smaller group who went out saying, "We have no king but Christ." These still enrich us, these still breathe upon us like the breath of an eternal springtime. Receiving power to live, they also received power to give. So it may be for us.

I think about the most needlessly cruel deed I ever witnessed took place at a Christmas celebration in our little village church. The tree must have been quite a crude affair, but to my boyish eyes it had the beauty of paradise. Santa Claus was present in person. We boys and girls gathered about him while he called our names and filled our hands with presents.

But there was one boy whose name was not called. He

was the village idiot. He stood with his ugly face turned toward the tree, one gaunt wistfulness. Then Santa Claus took down the largest box that was on the tree and called his name. He reached for his present with eager hands. He untied the string with fingers that trembled. Then he lifted the lid to find the box empty. Somebody, mistaking a tragedy for a joke, had given him only an empty box.

We are hanging presents upon the world's great Christmas tree, each of us. The presents we hang are the lives we live. Some give lives that are empty of goodness and empty of God. But it need not be so. It will certainly not be so for him who shares the faith of the disciples that Jesus is "the Christ, the Son of the living God" and receives this Christ into his own heart. This is the case because "he that believeth on me, . . . out of his inner life shall flow rivers of living water."

"Who say ye that I am?" To answer that question aright is to receive power to live and power to give.

BEING DECISIVE

Why call ye me, Lord, Lord, and do not the things which I say?

LUKE 6:46

This sane question is addressed to the undecided. In speaking to you on being decisive, I am speaking on a subject of major importance. This is an essential for successful living. If you know where you are going and are determined to get there, almost any old jalopy will serve the purpose. But if you cannot come to a definite decision as to your goal, then a Rolls-Royce will be of little avail. It would wear out and fall to pieces before you would reach your goal. Truly, for the ship that is bound for no harbor no wind can be favorable. No wonder, therefore, that our Lord is constantly calling us to be decisive: "Let your language be, 'Yes, yes,' or 'No, no'" (Weymouth).

How essential that is, and yet how difficult! So often our "Yes" has in it a tincture of "No," and our "No" a tincture of "Yes." To give utterance to a "Yes" that is one hundred percent affirmation is about the most difficult task that we are called upon to perform. The burden of choice is so heavy that many people go to pieces under it. There are young men who were happier in the army than they have ever been before or since. This is the case because there they were in some measure relieved of the burden of choice.

It is difficult to get people to think. It is more difficult still to get them to be decisive. What a keen thinker was Hamlet, Prince of Denmark! There are those who believe that the story of this prince is somewhat autobiographical. They believe that Hamlet, with his vast ability to think and his inability to act, is in a measure a picture of the poet himself. Be that as it may, Hamlet found action next to impossible. He did not like his situation. He rebelled at the fact that his world was out of joint and that he was ever born to set it right. He contemplated suicide, thought of it with brilliant clearness, but could never quite decide to go through with it:

> Who would fardels bear,
> To grunt and sweat under a weary life,
> But that the dread of something after death,
> The undiscover'd country from whose bourn
> No traveller returns, puzzles the will
> And makes us rather bear those ills we have
> Than fly to others that we know not of?
> Thus conscience does make cowards of us all;
> And thus the native hue of resolution
> Is sicklied o'er with the pale cast of thought,
> And enterprises of great pith and moment
> With this regard their currents turn awry,
> And lose the name of action.

I

Now look at this question of Jesus: "Why call ye me, Lord, Lord, and do not the things which I say?" We can readily realize the kind of folks to whom this question was addressed. Our Lord is not speaking to those who are out-and-out against him. He is not speaking to his avowed enemies, nor to those who ignore him. Neither is he speaking to those who are wholeheartedly for him. He is rather speaking to people very like many of us. He is speaking to those who admire him, who honor him to the point of calling him Lord, and yet who are not fully persuaded to follow him. They give him an intellectual assent, but have failed wholeheartedly to give him themselves.

Mark tells us of a man of this type. One day this man came to Jesus with this question: "Which is the first commandment of all?" When Jesus answered that the greatest commandment is to love God and man, his questioner approved his answer. In fact, he gave the answer of the Master such wise approval that Jesus commended him for his answer and then paid him this compliment: "Thou art not far from the kingdom of God." It was a beautiful commendation, and yet it was not enough. Though so near the kingdom that his foot was almost upon the threshold, he was not in it. One decisive step would have brought him to life's finest adventure, but, so far as we know, he failed to take that step.

Now this company of the undecided is a vast company. It is not uncharitable to say that it includes a large percentage of the members of our churches. This does not mean that these undecided folks are hypocritical. Very few of them are. It does not mean that they do not refrain from certain evils every day out of loyalty to Christ. It does not mean that they do not do certain deeds of service every day because of that loyalty. It does mean that, while they are obedient in many things, they still do not put the kingdom of God first. Though decent, religious, and respectable, there are areas in their lives that they have never dedicated to him whom they call Lord.

Not only does this company of the undecided include vast numbers who are in our churches, but it includes even more who are outside any church. As I have spoken to various clubs and organizations outside the church, I have discovered that it is by no means unpopular before such groups to sound a definitely religious note. Any reference to Jesus Christ, any word honoring him, is met with almost universal approval. Also, as I have spoken to men individually who were outside the church, I have found plenty of those who were harshly critical. These were often critical of the ministry. They could point out numerous flaws both in the church as a whole and in the individual members. But when I confessed that we were a faulty group, all of us, and then asked this question: "What about Jesus Christ? What fault have you to find in him?" I do not recall ever to have heard from these one harsh criticism. In spite of all our faults, there is a sense in which Jesus Christ is the most popular character in the United States today. Our tragedy is not that we are out-and-out against him; it is rather that we are not out-and-out for him.

II

"Why call ye me, Lord, Lord, and do not the things which I say?" Now, what is he asking at our hands? Let us get away from what is incidental to what is really essential.

To begin negatively, Jesus is not asking primarily for our church membership. By this I do not mean that it is not the duty of every Christian to belong to some church. I realize that there are many decent and right-thinking people outside the church. But it is my conviction that those who take Jesus seriously will join some church. The church at the time of Jesus was even more faulty than the church of today, yet Jesus did not stand apart from it and stone it. He rather attended it as a matter of habit and conviction. He knew that what help he brought he must bring as a member of the church and not as an outside antagonist.

Here and there I find people who have become too pious to belong to any church. I was preaching to a congregation some years ago in which was a brother who was giving me most encouraging backing by his hearty amens. Now, I approve of saying amen. When a hearer makes such a response I feel he is on my side. But this man overdid it. He was talking almost as fast as I was. By this I knew I had not yet rebuked his particular sin.

Then it happened. I said, "I believe in the church."

"Amen," was the response.

"Now and then," I continued, "I have found people who were too good to belong to any church."

"Amen."

"If I lived next door to a man like that," I continued, "I would lock my garage every night."

He started to say amen and it slid off like a feather-edged shingle. When the sermon was over I learned the truth. He had quit the church because the Lord had said, "Come out from among them and be ye separate." Personally I believe that if you take Jesus seriously you will join some church. But our Lord is not asking for that first of all.

No more is Jesus asking first for our work. Of course, if we are in earnest about following him, we are certain to do something about it. But his first demand is not for our work. Neither is he seeking first for our money. Naturally if our Christianity is real we shall be glad to give, but money does not come first. No more is our Lord asking for some kind of emotional response. He is seeking neither for our laughter nor our tears. For what then,

I repeat, is he asking? He is asking for ourselves. He is saying to us what he said to Matthew long ago: "Follow me." This publican was decisive. He at once left all, rose up, and followed. This also we are to do. Jesus is asking what Paul urged in these words: "Present your bodies a living sacrifice." He is asking for our complete and unconditional dedication of life. Nothing less than that will meet his demands.

If you think that sounds difficult I am ready to agree. Jesus never hinted that discipleship was easy. But when he set out to redeem us he did not seek an easy way. He took the way of the cross. "This is my body," he declares, "which is given for you." "This," he is saying, "is myself, my very all, my everything, and it is given for you." He asks that in return we take our discipleship seriously. As he gave his all, we are to give our all. We are to say day by day, "Not my will but thine be done."

III

Why should we do this?

1. We ought to be wholehearted in our decision because nothing else will satisfy our Lord. He is never pleased with halfhearted devotion. In fact, it would seem, as we turn the pages of the New Testament, that that is just the attitude that he hates most. He even prefers out-and-out antagonism: "I would thou wert cold or hot." What are we here to do? Not to win success primarily. Certainly we are not here to fail. We are here to do the will of God. It is only by a wholehearted dedication to him that we can please him and thus fulfill God's purpose for our lives.

2. It is only by our wholehearted loyalty that we can

find satisfaction for ourselves. There is no peace for the undecided. The most wretched hours of our lives are those hours when we are unable to reach a decision. Even a wrong decision brings more peace than does indecision. The wise story of Jonah emphasizes this fact.

Listen to this: "The word of the Lord came unto Jonah . . . saying, Arise, go to Nineveh, that great city, and cry against it." There were two possibilities open to this prophet: to go or not to go. He decided against the call of God. We have that amazing power. Having reached a definite decision to renounce God by disobeying him, he went on shipboard and fell fast asleep. The days and nights that had preceded his decision had been full of agony. When he at last decided, even though his decision was wrong, that decision brought sufficient peace to make sleep possible.

But the trouble with the peace born of a wrong decision is that it will not last. This is the case because God simply will not let us alone. He refuses to leave off his loving efforts to win us. "No man can be as bad as he wants to be." We may reject the high calling of God, but our rejection will bring us no permanent peace. It is only when we have fully committed ourselves to God that we come to know the peace that abides.

Then a wholehearted decision to follow Christ brings peace because so many lesser questions are decided by it. There are those for whom no moral issue is finally decided. Every morning they must decide whether they will pray or not pray, whether they will look into God's Word or neglect it. Every Sunday church attendance is an open question. These people are therefore in constant conflict. They remind one of that old story of the man who possessed a dog whose tail was far too long, but, desiring to give the dog the least possible pain, he decided to cut it off an inch a day rather than all at once. If you take Jesus seriously a thousand lesser decisions will then be made in advance.

Not only will this one great decision include many that are smaller, but it will make every other right decision easier. The choice you made today was born quite largely of the choice you made yesterday. Every wrong choice makes the next wrong choice the easier and the surer. When Rip Van Winkle used to swear off drinking he would return to his bottle saying, "I will not count this one." But even if he failed to count it, his weakened will did not. It chalked that failure against him. Now, just as every wrong choice makes the next wrong choice easier, even so every right choice makes the next right choice easier and surer. We can so cultivate our right choices in the fellowship of Jesus that they become all but spontaneous.

3. Then we ought to be fully decided in the matter of following Christ, because this alone brings us to our highest usefulness. Indecision means weakness. Years ago when we were boys, my brother and I in passing through the fields had to cross a spring branch which was normally two or three feet wide. But heavy rains had given this little stream a breadth of from ten to fifteen feet. In spite of this we decided we could jump it. I was to adventure first. So I gave myself a good running start and was on the way to victory when my brother changed his mind and shouted, "Stop! Stop! Stop!" The result was that I lost my decisiveness. The further result was that I landed in the middle of the stream. But my failure was not due to my lack of athletic ability. It was due rather to my indecision.

In those dark days when Israel was being swept off its feet by Jezebel, it was Elijah who saved the day. Standing before a great throng he flung at them this sane question: "How long halt ye between two opinions?" In other words, "How long are you going to allow yourselves to be crippled by your indecision?" To be thus undecided is as silly as trying to win a foot race with a ball and chain on your ankle. Indecision brings weakness. Decision brings strength.

Years ago I watched a company of men move the side of a mountain. They were not using bulldozers as we do today. They were using hydraulic pressure. When that water fell from the heavens it doubtless fell so gently that it would hardly have hurt a baby's face. But now, under its tremendous pressure, small trees were being uprooted and rocks were being pushed out of their places. Why the difference? This water was saying, "This one thing I do." It is only as we are wholeheartedly for Christ that we find our highest personal satisfaction and highest usefulness.

4. Then we ought to decide definitely for Christ, because by refusing to do so we decide against him. There is a fable that a donkey once stood between two delicious bundles of hay. The donkey was hungry. Both bundles offered just the satisfaction he needed. But when he would turn toward the one, the other would seem to call to him. Thus he could never make up his mind just which bundle he would eat first. Therefore he hesitated between the two until he starved. His death was not the result of a decision to commit suicide. It was rather the result of his failure to decide to eat.

Even so we miss knowing Jesus Christ through lack of decision. Right now he is offering himself to us. Most of us have declared to him our allegiance in some fashion. But, in spite of this, some of us are keenly conscious of the fact that our religious lives often have been quite disappointing. We wonder at times if we had not better renounce the whole venture as a failure. What is the way to victory? Make a wholehearted decision. God longs to give you the best, but he cannot without your cooperation. Remember that God's one plan of salvation is for a surrendered heart.